Unfair

Uriah the Hittite's Life of Service

John Wesley Rowe, Jr.

Unfair
Uriah the Hittite's Life of Service
Copyright © 2015 by John Wesley Rowe, Jr.

Request for information should be addressed to:
John Wesley Rowe, Jr.
wesleyrowe@earthlink.net

ISBN-13:
978-0692415627
ISBN-10:
0692415629
Library of Congress Catalogue Number: 2015905060
BISAC: Religion / Biblical Commentary / General

All scripture quotations, unless otherwise indicated are taken from the King James Version of the Bible.

Use that does not require written permission: Text from other versions of the Bible are quoted utilizing the industry standard that in any form (written, visual, electronic or audio), up to and inclusive of 500 verses or less without written permission, providing the verses quoted do not amount to a complete book of the Bible, nor do verses quoted account for 25% or more of the total text of the work in which they are quoted, and the verses are not being quoted in a commentary or other biblical reference work. This permission is contingent upon an appropriate copyright acknowledgment. Used by permission, the Authorized King James Version of the Bible, Copyright © 1966 used by permission of Zondervan Publishing House. All rights reserved worldwide. Used by permission Holy Bible: The Living Translation, Copyright © 1966. Used by permission of Tyndale House Publishers, Inc. Wheaton, IL 60189. Used by permission The New King James Version, Thomas-Nelson Publishers, Copyright © 1975.

Quotations within publishing industry standards are also taken from: Thomas, M. W. (1964). The Mystery of Godliness. Zondervan Publishing House. Use by permission of Zondervan. Thomas, M. I. (1961). The Saving Life of Christ, Zondervan Publishing House. Thomas, M. I. (1961). The Saving Life of Christ, Zondervan Publishing House. Use by permission of Zondervan. Barnhouse, Donald Grey, (1965) The Invisible War, Zondervan Publishing House. Use by permission of Zondervan. Sprague, W. B. (1839). The Life and Sermons of Edward D. Griffin. Carlisle, PA: First Banner of Truth edition 1987.

All rights reserved. No portion of this publication may be reproduced, stored in a retrieval system, or transmitted in any form or by any means-electronic, mechanical, photocopy, recording, or any other except for brief quotations in printed reviews, without the prior permission of the publisher/author.

Cover designed by Bethany Joy Rowe

Cover photograph by Patricia Rowe

Printed in the United States of America

Contents

Unfair
Uriah the Hittites Life of Service

Acknowledgements		
Prologue:	Why write a book on Uriah the Hittite?	1
One:	What is in the name Uriah?	11
Two:	What is the meaning of a Hittite ancestry?	23
Three:	The Curse on the Hittites	29
Four:	Uriah the Hittite is a dead man walking	35
Five:	A change in name for his people.	49
Six:	How to become one of David's mighty men?	55
Seven:	It is the worst of times.	63
Eight:	The devil is about to drive	72
Nine:	The worst of times are about to get worse.	81
Ten:	The country is full of cancer	89
Eleven:	When a King rejects placing faith in God...	97
Twelve:	When Saul's cancer metastasizes...	105
Thirteen:	When he enters David's camp...	113
Fourteen:	A man who knows God supplies...	113
Fifteen:	A man with a band of brothers...	135
Sixteen:	Location, location, location....	145
Seventeen:	A man is right in his own eyes....	151
Eighteen:	When his trophy bride reveals her colors...	157
Nineteen:	Evil at play in high places?	163
Twenty:	Is Uriah's marriage a forerunner of Hosea?	171
Twenty-One:	Is Uriah's wife Bathsheba raped....	181
Twenty-Two:	Is the scandalous affair flaunted...	191
Twenty-Three:	With the knowledge of his wife....	201
Twenty-Four:	What does a living sacrifice do...	215
Twenty-Five:	After adultery with his wife....	223
Twenty-Six:	The last shall be first	231
Bibliography		239

Acknowledgments

As with most of us, our lives are often shaped by the people with whom and the events in which we walk through life. Many events and relationships in our lives can result in incredible pain. Often this pain is the results of how circumstances outside our control impact us. From a human perspective these events may often seem terribly unfair, completely unjustifiable, and totally underserved. This book is dedicated to my wife Kay who has tread with me through life's blessings, trials and hardships and continues to stand by me.

It is my desire to walk readers through my study of the life of Uriah the Hittite. His life from an earthly perspective was unfair and a complete rip-off. Uriah lived a life of Godly service that would be the envy of any Christian, yet everything of earthly value was systematically stripped from him.

Uriah's national leaders were men who turned their backs on God. Uriah was stripped of family and friends by the genocidal efforts of King Saul. His many years of loyal service to his boss King David garnered him no enduring honor. King David took advantage of his power and position to engage in adultery with Uriah's wife Bathsheba while Uriah was at work doing his boss's bidding. Uriah's wife easily yields to King David's sexual advances while her husband was away on business. An unwanted pregnancy results from the adulterous philandering. Uriah is robbed of his life by his murderous King David, so the King could hide his sin.

This story is ostensibly a murder mystery, yet everyone knows the end of the story. The mystery this book attempts to explain is how and why it all happens. The journey covers the genealogy and history surrounding Uriah the Hittite and other key players in this story.

My life has also been tremendously influenced by one of life's most difficult challenges, the death of a child. The death of a child is a spiritual challenge that no Christian wants, but it is the unfathomable sacrifice that God the Father took upon Himself when putting redemption's plan in place.

I have also been touched by the writings of Rev. Edward Dorr Griffin who had great influence on America's Second Great Awakening. Griffin's treatise The Doctrine of Divine Efficiency, Defended Against Certain Modern Speculations reveals how America has slipped into doctrines not firmly founded in God's Word. These scriptural departures have caused many in American churches difficulty when addressing life's tragedies.

Uriah's underpinning in this book is divine efficiency. It is the effectual power of God immediately applied to the heart to make it holy. Our God is a sovereign God, and we are sheep in His pasture.

As Martin Luther put it in <u>A Mighty Fortress</u>:

Did we in our own strength confide, our striving would be losing;
Were not the right Man on our side, the Man of God's own choosing:
Dost ask who that may be? Christ Jesus, it is He;
Lord Sabaoth, His Name, from age to age the same,
And He must win the battle.

The free will struggle of modern theology is a striving that is losing. Luther has it right when in the third stanza of that great hymn when he speaks, "We will not fear, for God hath willed His truth to triumph through us." Philippians 2:13 says, "For it is God who worketh in you, both to will and to do of His good pleasure." God speaks into a man's heart and his only charge and choice is just do the shepherd's bidding.

I have a friend Dr. Edward Eastman. Dr. Eastman provided untold insight and assistance in editing this book. Dr. Eastman was not always in agreement with this former investigative reporter's conclusions. But we are but threads in God's great tapestry, and I am eternally grateful for the moments the

Weaver's shuttle brought our threads together in the writing of this book and in life.

I would also like to thank Rev. Jeff Brewer and Rev. Larry Briggs for reading my manuscript prior to publication and offering valuable input. Ed, Jeff and Larry are and always will be predestined to eternally be my friends.

John Wesley Rowe, Jr.

Prologue:

Why write a book on Uriah the Hittite?

I have had a number of events in my life that the world would consider unfair. I have been passed over for promotions due to nepotism. In one instance a competitor for an envied position within the company covered up moral lapses for a high ranking company executive and received the promotion. But the most unfair event to date in my life was the death of my second son, and it is this unfair story covered by God's grace that birthed the writing of this book.

"That the trial of your faith, being much more precious than of gold that perisheth, though it be tried with fire, might be found unto praise and honour and glory at the appearing of Jesus Christ," says 1 Peter 1:7. (KJV)

The two words, trial and tried, Peter uses are tough words. The words speak to the proving and the proof of our faith. It is a hard thing this testing of our faith. The currency is life. A passing grade requires death to our old nature. Being a living sacrifice is our reasonable service. And the reward is eternal.

Thirty years ago my wife and I went to the hospital for the birth of our second child. We had waited over two years to conceive this son. My wife's first delivery was very difficult. Over thirty hours of labor ended with a caesarian section.

This second birth would also to be a caesarian section. C-sections are scheduled, tidy and quick for a father. Indeed, what remained cemented in my mind about our first son's birth is a c-section's speed. After thirty hours of labor the doctor and nurses hauled my wife into the operating room, and I had a son in about 15 minutes.

The second pregnancy had gone well. The heartbeat was strong. The ultra sound was problem free. No indication of the sudden and unexpected turn in our lives presented itself.

We arrived early at the hospital. The c-section was scheduled for mid-morning. I stayed with Kay until the gurney broke the doors to the operating room. This hospital didn't allow fathers in the operating room for c-sections.

I went to the surgery waiting room. It was the same waiting room I visited two years prior. This was the second time around. I was an old pro. I checked my watch. Ten minutes, fifteen tops and I would see my newborn. C-sections are quick I repeated to myself.

But ten minutes became fifteen. Fifteen minutes became twenty. Thirty minutes became forty-five. Something was terribly wrong, I could feel it. Finally a nurse turned the corner and walked toward the waiting room.

My greatest fears were confirmed. As the nurse approached I could see tears streaming down her face. She wipes the tears away with a tissue, but it was too late.

Your wife is OK the nurse said, but your son is having a very difficult time. The doctor wants to see you immediately.

We moved quickly down the hallway and through the heavy metal doors that sheltered the outside world from my son's life and death struggle.

My wife and I had already decided to name our son Joshua which is the Old Testaments render of the name Jesus. From the intensity being exhibited by the medical team surrounding my Joshua, I judged the situation desperate.

It was explained to me that the doctor working on Joshua was the one of the leading neo-natal pediatrician in the mid-west. He just happened to be in the hospital at the time. The nurse assured me that everything possible was being done to help our son.

Joshua had what appeared to be huge needles in his wrists. The sterile steel looked like stakes next to his tiny newborn hands. His lower legs suffered the same fate as his wrists. I thought to myself, his arms and legs ought to be enough, why do they have one of those things stuck in his side.

Joshua was coughing, struggling to breathe. Even with the assistance of all the finest technology, nothing seemed to be helping.

The doctor, who had remained hovered over my son, stopped and straightened up. He looked in my direction and walked to me.

In a matter of fact fashion the doctor said, "Your son is going to die. What would you have us do? His lungs have not developed properly, and as long as he stayed in the womb he was fine. But it is impossible for him to breathe on his own."

What was I to say? I was far too young in my faith to lay hands on Joshua and pray for healing.

I reached over and touch him as he struggled for life. The nurse, with all the love in the world, wrapped Joshua in a blanket for me.

I sat in a rocker in the neo-natal intensive care unit. Joshua and I rocked until I knew he had passed. Tears were running down my face. What was I to tell my wife when she awoke from the anesthetic?

But I did not have to tell my wife. The Holy Spirit had already visited her. Begging prayers were being followed by bitter tears. The answer was no.

The Holy Spirit provided the necessary strength for us to overcome the first days following our son's death. It remains miraculous to me for I knew the strength was not mine.

My wife and I consoled each other. One of my most difficult tasks was sharing with our first born son John that Joshua wouldn't be coming home with mom from the hospital. John's months of listening to his mom read to him and his unborn brother and John's amazement in watching his brother kick around inside his mother's tummy made this life very real to him. When I told John that his little brother Joshua had gone to live with Jesus in heaven, he said he didn't understand. Neither did I.

I made the funeral arrangements.

My wife insisted that I purchase special thank you cards for all the doctors and nurses that had provided her care. She was ministering to those who had helped her. Her actions were a testament to the Holy Spirit's indwelling. She could not have exhibited such peace in the face of such sorrow were it not for Jesus Christ.

But in the weeks to come, we faced our demons.

Why us!

After about three weeks life returned to what now seemed mundane. The calls and cards had come to an end. We were left with our private thoughts. The miraculous strength with which we had been empowered faded. The glory that had shown on our faces flickered ever dimmer. The pain of the empty arms made minutes seem like hours.

"Lord, we wanted Joshua," I cried. "God, people are killing babies by the millions in abortion clinics. Why did you take our son? Why have you punished us?"

A work related meeting required me to make a long commute. While returning from that trip my anger with God overflowed. I was shouting at God in my car as I drove homeward. If you loved me God, you wouldn't have done this to me.

The next words were nearly audible in my car. To this day I remain uncertain as to whether or not I actually heard The Father speak to me with my ears or whether the Holy Spirit so vividly painted the words on my heart that I only thought the words were spoken.

"Wes, do you remember those needles stuck in your Joshua's arms and legs? Do you remember that needle stuck in your Joshua's side?

Those working on your Joshua were trying to save his life. Those steel needles were thrust into his hands, feet and sides in an effort to save him. You would have done anything to make it all right for your Joshua. But you couldn't.

Now you have a small taste of what I felt when the nails were driven through My Joshua's hands and feet and when the spear pierced his side.

The difference between your love and My love is you couldn't stop what happened to your Joshua. I could have stopped what was happening to My Joshua, but I didn't.

Your Joshua is with me now. I sacrificed My Son, so you could become my son, and in time you will be able to spend eternity with your son. Now, don't put what I have taught you in a closet."

A revival started in our small Southern Baptist church after Joshua's passing. The church's compassion flowed into a healing ministry for hurting pastors. The small little church became a sanctuary and refuge for hurting men and women of God.

A year passed. My wife had summoned the courage to bear another child. Our third son was born. He was a healthy child. He was born in the same hospital that we had left thirteen months before with empty arms. People at the hospital had not forgotten Kay's testimony from the previous year when our Joshua died. The same nurse who shed tears of grief coming for me in the waiting room the previous year burst into our room with tears of joy.

Psalm 30:5 For his anger endureth but a moment; in his favour [is] life: weeping may endure for a night, but joy cometh in the morning. (KJV)

Yet another year passed. I had received a promotion that required relocation and training. The training occurred in Orlando, Florida, so as a family we traveled to Florida. I attended training. My wife hung out at the hotel pool with our four year old and one year old sons.

Our youngest son has curly hair. While he was a baby his hair was soft and bushy. I being a child of the 1960's liked longer hair on my boys. So our young curly headed kid was occasionally mistaken for a girl.

One evening while we were in Orlando I returned to the hotel room for dinner. One of my fellow class members was a local and had recommended at steak house near our hotel. I had tasted that steak the entire afternoon. I went into our room and announced that we were going out for steaks at great place a local recommended.

My wife said she wasn't feeling well, and she wanted to go to a nationwide chain cafeteria near our hotel so she could get green beans. Can you imagine it? Green beans in lieu of a juicy steak! I had a fit. She insisted on the chain cafeteria for green beans. I was honked. I really dislike eating at a cafeteria. But I was hungry, so we were off to cafeteria.

The lines were very long. We were being herded back and forth between velvet covered ropes. This place had taken a lesson in Orlando theme park crowd control. I still wanted a steak, and the situation was beginning to annoy me greatly.

A forlorn looking young lady kept watching our bushy headed youngest son. As we shuffled past each other during one turn of the ropes the young lady asked how old our little girl was. My wife explained that the little girl was actually a little boy with a father who didn't believe in haircuts. My wife asked the young lady about her family. The young lady shared with stunning frankness in this crowded foyer that her baby daughter died the previous week from a rare genetic disorder. The disorder would have a one in four chance of being passed on to any future children she might have.

My wife in just as matter of fact tone shared that she had also lost a son two years ago. The noisy entryway had become uncharacteristically quiet. We passed each other several more times as we weaved our way through the ropes. The ladies continued their conversation with each passing. The surrounding crowd pressed to listen as these two young women shared with each other how God had revealed Himself through the trials. But this young lady was filled with fear about having another child because of the possibility of passing the genetic disorder onto that child. My wife shared how she overcame like fears.

It was time for my family to slide our trays, so the conversations with this couple came to an end. This cafeteria had a hostess that seated customers. The customers didn't pick their own seats. She seated the customers at her discretion. But my wife didn't feel the conversation with this hurting young woman was finished. In all my spirituality I said if God wants us to continue our conversation with this couple then He will bring them over here and have them seated next to us.

My wife kept an eye out for this couple, but there was nowhere within shouting distance for them to dine near our table. My wife spotted the couple as they exited the food line. The hostess moved to seat the exiting couple. As if verbally commanded by God, the family at the table next to ours stood up in unison and exited quickly. A bus boy was standing next to the table, and he cleaned the table with amazing speed and precision. The hostess greeted the couple, turned, saw the table next to ours being prepared and headed our way. I looked at my wife and said, "I guess God wants us to continue our conversation."

We spent a great deal of time talking with this couple. The husband was an airline pilot and the wife was a homemaker. We discovered the couple lived minutes from my mother-in-law. We had planned to spend the next week with my mother-in-law, so my wife arranged a visit with the couple. During that meeting my wife continued to encourage her kindred spirit to bear another child. The young woman tried again, and about a year later she gave birth to a baby free from any genetic disorder on Easter Sunday. The woman's church followed her nine month journey of faith. With the healthy birth of her child their church experienced a revival of God's love.

So the trials of life have good purpose. Situations like the event mentioned above have occurred several times through our lives. Trials are not just to be endured and placed as dusty memories in a closet. Endured trials are the proof of our faith. Like Uriah the Hittite we must utilize that proof for its intended purpose. Though some trials may seem more than a person can bear, well done thou good and faithful servant awaits those who finish the race of faith.

God will continue to use the trials of your life. These seemingly tragic events are often filled with more anguish than a person believes they can carry. But the healing comes when we take our eyes off our own pain and look to the service of others. To help others overcome is the reason for Joshua's life and that is the reason for this book.

And if you don't believe God's timing is perfect just imagine if our trip to the cafeteria had been delayed a few seconds longer. My wife and I would not have passed the couple she so caringly served as we were herded through the velvet ropes. There are no coincidences with our God.

Chapter One

What is in the name Uriah?

What can be said of a man whose name and whose life is overshadowed by his wife's adulterous affair with a philandering King David. The liaison between Bathsheba, Uriah the Hittite's wife, and his boss King David results in a child. An elaborate plan is hatched then botched in an attempt to cover up the paternal identity of a problem unwanted pregnancy. Finally the leader of a nation in a complete abuse of the power and privileges of his God given office arranges the murder of a loyal servant and faithful husband to save his own reputation!

Uriah the Hittite is an individual whose identity has been stolen. Uriah, the living breathing man, is defined in human history by his murderer's heinous conspiratorial act. Yet Uriah lived an extraordinary life and what an extraordinary death he died. His earthly reputation, fame and glory has been laid aside like a fallen memorial stone in an ancient graveyard. Though covered and overgrown by years of neglect, with care the monument can be restored. The faded and worn stone can once again see the light of day and stand-up to examination.

The inscription on a burial stone calls out a name. It identifies and brings to mind the bearer of the name. It is an invitation to dig into the essence of the soul that bears that moniker. Uriah the Hittite is a name worthy of exploration and discovery.

Yet often an identity established through a life wonderfully lived is overshadowed by the context of a horrific death. The vitality of a vibrantly lived life is lost in the grievous nature of the person's passing. The recent memories of two American journalists beheaded by Islamic jihadists exemplify lives overshadowed by cruel murderous deaths.

A precious or notable life far too often is defined by history through the untimely nature of its end. And so it has far too often been with the biblical history of Uriah the Hittite. To live the life and die the death that fulfills God's plan and destiny for that life is as it should be.

To live the life God meant for you to live and to die the death God ordained you to die is the roll of a faithful servant. God has chosen the thread each servant is to walk, so the greater purpose of the Father's divine tapestry can be woven. An individual thread in God's tapestry can lose sight of the tapestry's finished beauty when the thread has eyes only on itself.

David was Uriah's king. David was Uriah's commander in chief and battlefield general. David was a leader who sent his army to war as he fritted away his days sleeping as his soldiers went into harm's way. David was an adulterous predator whose voyeurism soiled Uriah's bride. Bathsheba's easily yielded virtue signed Uriah's death warrant. The sin of others stole Uriah's identity or did it?

The memory of Uriah the Hittite's life is far too often half told. Couched in Sunday school lessons focusing on the events leading to the forcible taking of his life we often think of Uriah as a dup, a sod or an out of touch zealot blind to his circumstance. Who is this mighty man? What is a Hittite anyway? The Bible testifies to the nature of this honorable and faithful servant of the Most High God, and with an open heart a faithful reader of God's Word can find the real Uriah the Hittite.

Much can be discovered through the examination of Uriah's name and the life into which he was put by God. As the late Major Ian Thomas said, (Thomas, 1964) God has put us all in different places in this world. Some are pastors, others farmers, doctors, teachers, attorneys, clerks, builders, mothers, and fathers. But we must never forget that where we are put is not our job as Christians. Our job is to know God and let God be God in us and through us, so the world will look at us and say I need a little of what that guy or that gal has going on in their life. Do you share the saving grace of the Christ through a simple smile, with an unsolicited kind word, with a gift of a few dollars to someone in a time of need?

Christ's love can be expressed to this world even with both hands tied behind the back. A man or women, boy or girl can do it even if they feel as if they are nothing more than a flea with no resources and of so little account that their lot in life is to live on the butt end of the family dog, suck his blood and make him scratch.

But God can use every man, women and child within the circumstances He has placed and has established them even though the world may say that that individual has a flea's lot in life. God used Uriah and He wants to use every Christian. It is a Christian's spiritual heritage. How can such a thing be said? I say it because it is what God says. The Apostle Paul shares in his letter to the Ephesians chapter 1 verses 11-12, "In whom also we have obtained an inheritance being predestinated according to the purpose of him who worketh all things after the counsel of his own will: That we should be to the praise of his glory, who first trusted in Christ." (KJV)

To set some ground work for the validity of our exploration of Uriah the Hittite's name, let us visit the third chapter of Nehemiah and the 25th verse.

For those who don't remember the story Nehemiah has returned to Jerusalem with a remnant from the Babylonian exile. The remnant is in the process of rebuilding the city walls, and this chapter is the graveyard for the spiritual heritage of those involved in this rebuilding process. These folks are known by their stones not unlike the remembrances recorded on stones today in our modern graveyards and not unlike Uriah's murder.

This chapter of Nehemiah for the most part describes who was put where. Their work for the Lord was rebuilding the wall around Jerusalem. No section of the wall was any more important than any other. If the wall wasn't complete the enemy could pour into the city through the breach or gap. Nothing done had value until all was finished. So where you were put in the wall rebuilding process was insignificant when compared with finishing the job. So this chapter describes where folks were put.

Nehemiah 3.25 says "Palal the son of Uzai, over against the turning of the wall, and the tower which lieth out from the king's high house, that was by the court of the prison. After him Pedaiah the son of Parosh." (KJV)

At first blush this verse is not what could be called a John 3:16. No high profile athlete is painting this verse on a piece of athletic gear to drive curious sports fans to their Bibles. No eager fan is holding up a placard hoping a television camera catches a glimpse of Nehemiah 3:25 during an extra point conversion attempt at a national televised professional football game. Perhaps in the drudgery of a through the entire Bible reading effort you pretended to scan this jewel in the rough. Palal the son of Uzai, Pedaiah the son of Parosh, I can hear the casual Bible reader sputtering, "Why cannot these guys have normal names like John, Juan, Jean or Giovanni?"

Well, Pedaiah is a great name. It says something about what this family thought about their God. Pedaiah means "Jehovah has ransomed." (Strong) God has ransomed each one of us for a price. As Christians we know the ransom paid by God the Father. God the Father provided the life of his Son as a ransom for The Church. It is the old redemption story.

But whose son was Pedaiah the son of Parosh. The name Parosh means flea. Jehovah has ransomed the son of Flea, a blood sucking disease carrying parasite. So if God ransomed the son of a flea to rebuild the walls of Jerusalem, he certainly can use every man, women and child called according to His purpose to rebuild the walls of their lives even though they may feel like their address remains on the butt end of the family dog. Remember, Jerusalem's walls even had a dung gate where all city excrement was taken, and someone rebuilt the sewage treatment gate.

So there is much to be learned from names, genealogies and nationalities of those recorded in the Bible. Uriah's name is coupled with his nationality which speaks to his family's ancestral roots. So looking under the Hittite rocks for all the generic missing Uriah relatives is a genealogical search worthy of pursuit.

Before chasing after the Hittite in Uriah the Hittite, the meaningfulness of the name Uriah needs exploration and discovery. The name Uriah translates to the flame of Jehovah, or

Jehovah is my light or flame. Do you get the idea that lights come on when Uriah is around?

Think of all the times when God spoke in, through and with flames. Let's go back to the beginning at the Garden of Eden. Adam and Eve ate from the Tree of the Knowledge of Good and Evil. Eating from this forbidden fruit was the fall of men and women into sin. God initiated the process of redemption, and Adam and Eve were ejected from the Garden of Eden. God sent a significant message that this couple could not return to the Garden of Eden in their own strength.

Genesis 3:23-24 says, "Therefore the LORD God sent him forth from the garden of Eden, to till the ground from whence he was taken. So he drove out the man; and he placed at the east of the garden of Eden Cherubim, and a flaming sword which turned every way, to keep the way of the tree of life." (KJV)

Here is an eviction notice posted and punctuated by two cherubim carrying huge flaming swords. As is the case today, eviction notices are usually delivered by an armed sheriff. Adam and Eve did not want to leave this most wonderful home, yet the couple knew they had placed their interest ahead of the landlord. The relationship with the landlord of Eden had been broken. As the case in evictions today a show of legal force is frequently required to remove those who have failed in their contractual relationship with the landlord. The broken covenant requires new lines to be drawn in the relationship. So God drove them out of the garden because the couple was no longer worthy of service in an unsoiled place.

God sent Adam and Eve to the soil, to the earth, to the ground. The couple was not abandoned and totally cut off without hope like the fallen angels ejected from heaven with Satan. Yet as a reminder of their lost innocence and of their complete inability to return to the bliss of the Garden of Eden stands the cherubim holding the undeniable power of the flaming swords.

So Uriah the Hittite, the flame of Jehovah, has a name that packs a punch. Flames do have biblical significance. What can be gleaned from Moses's burning bush that might provide more insight into this name Uriah, flame of Jehovah? When and where did the flames find their way into Moses's life and is there a correlation to Uriah's life? But most importantly why did the flames come to Moses?

Exodus 3.1-3 says. "Now Moses kept the flock of Jethro his father in law, the priest of Midian: and he led the flock to the backside of the desert, and came to the mountain of God, even to Horeb. And the angel of the LORD appeared unto him in a flame of fire out of the midst of a bush: and he looked, and, beholds, the bush burned with fire, and the bush was not consumed. And Moses said, I will now turn aside, and see this great sight, why the bush is not burnt." (KJV)

Let us remember that Moses was tending his father-in-law's flocks on the far side of the desert. Moses was raised as a Prince of Egypt. If an Ivy League education existed in the ancient world it was found in Egypt and as a member of the royal family every benefit there unto appertaining was extended to Moses. He was trained up as a leader of men, and men extended Moses every respect at the penalty of death.

Yet where do we find Moses when the flame manifests? Moses is found on the backside of the desert.

Many Christian men and women find themselves in a position much the same as Moses. As the economic recession continues to rock the United States thousands of Christians find themselves on the backside of their own deserts. Millions in the United States today find themselves unemployed or like Moses underemployed. The benefits of their hard work, the advanced degrees that highlight their curriculum vitae, the networks of powerful friends have been found hollow in this economy. The prestige of closing the million dollar deal around a fortune 500 boardroom, the Mac Mansion to lay one's head down at night, the awe of your neighbors when you arrive home in the new chariot has all evaporated in this economy. Thousands find their mortgages underwater. The Ivy League educated are working five or six part-time jobs. Personal actualization has turned into alienation. Many are being forced to move back home and live with mom and dad or the in-laws just like Moses.

Moses had been in this situation for quite a few years. The accolades of men have been replaced by the bleating of sheep. The only green to be found bulging from Moses' wallet was a few extra handfuls of grass for the baby lambs.

God has left many reassigned to new situations, and often many are finding it difficult to receive the new orders graciously. It is important to note that Moses did not seem to be put off by his lapse into obscurity, and he showed no sign or desire to extract himself from his situation.

Philippians 4:11 says. "Not that I speak in respect of want: for I have learned, in whatsoever state I am, therewith to be content." (KJV) and 1Timothy 6:6-8 shares, "But godliness with contentment is great gain. For we brought nothing into this world, and it is certain we can carry nothing out. And having food and raiment let us be there with content."(KJV) It is incredibly difficult to receive more from God when contentment with our current state is not to be found.

But Moses found himself in a contented state. When Moses saw the burning bush his mind was not distracted by the cares of this world. Far too often when God speaks to a discontented Christian they hear His voice but turn aside to more important issues of their choice and direction. But Moses was not distracted by competing voices. He turned from what he was doing and took a closer look at this flame that did not consume the bush that it burned. A huge bomb fire was not required to attract a contented Moses. It was the curiosity of the nature of the fire that drew Moses to a closer look.

Psalms 73:28 says "But it is good for me to draw near to God: I have put my trust in the Lord GOD, that I may declare all thy works."(KJV) God speaks in unusual ways and often says things that turn our worlds inside out.

The "flame of the Lord" spoke through Elijah numerous times. In 1King 18:37-39 the Old Testament records, "Hear me, O LORD, hear me, that this people may know that thou art the LORD God, and that thou hast turned their heart back again. Then the fire of the LORD fell, and consumed the burnt sacrifice, and the wood, and the stones, and the dust, and licked up the water that was in the trench. And when all the people saw it, they fell on their faces: and they said, The LORD, he is the God; the LORD, he is the God."(KJV) So God has produced conviction, repentance and action when He speaks with flames.

In Acts 2.2-4 The Holy Spirit arrives dressed in flames. "And there appeared unto them cloven tongues like as of fire, and it sat upon each of them. And they were all filled with the Holy Ghost, and began to speak with other tongues, as the Spirit gave them utterance."(KJV) In the New Covenant the flame consumes men without burning them or consuming them. As servants of I AM THAT I AM Christians become the scruffy desert bush that is not consumed as the cloven tongues of fire sit on and cover but do not consume. As Christians we speak God's words to a lost world through the flaming words the indwelling Holy Spirit chooses to speak from and through the lips of the born again believer.

What incredible images are wrapped up in the name Uriah, the flame of the Lord? Events in Uriah's life reveal God's use of this mighty man as His flame to speak to men. Indeed Uriah's life does speak to all who turn aside and see this great sight, the great testimony that is his life of servitude.

But Uriah is only half of the name on this escutcheon. Unlike Pedaiah we are not told that Uriah's father is a blood sucking parasite named Flea. We are not told who Uriah's father is, but we are told what Uriah's father is. Uriah was born of a Hittite, and according to God's command all Hittites should have been dead.

Chapter Two

What is the meaning of a Hittite ancestry?

Wherever the written Word of God has a gravestone, that marker will carry significant information about the person or people that bear its weight. The first mention of the Hittite as a people group appears in Genesis chapter twenty-three. Sarah, the beloved wife of Abraham has died at one hundred twenty-seven years in Kirjatharba in the land of Canaan. The town of Kirjatharba will later in the Bible be called Hebron. In fact nearly all Old Testament mentions of Hittite people reference this band of folks living in or about this southern Palestine area known as Hebron.

Abraham was distraught at the passing of his wife, and he wailed and lamented her passing which is a quite appropriate act after having been married to her for over a century. After shedding great tears of mourning Abraham ends his tribute beside his wife's corpse, and as men and women have done throughout time stands and proceeds with making the arrangements for Sarah's interment.

In this land of Canaan dwelled the sons of Heth. Abraham directs his attention to a group of locals who had apparently gather upon hearing of the passing of the great man's wife. Abraham says, "I am a stranger and a sojourner with you: give me a possession of a burying place with you, that I may bury my dead out of my sight."(KJV)

In Matthew 20:16, Luke 13:30 and Mark 10:31 Jesus says, "But many that are first shall be last; and the last first."(KJV) The Godly principle that the first shall be last and the last shall be first starts to manifest in Uriah's heritage with these ancestral Hittites. Matthew Henry's commentary shares, "Our Lord added, that everyone who had forsaken possessions or comforts, for his sake and the gospel, would be recompensed at last. May God give us faith to rest our hope on this his promise; then we shall be ready for every service or sacrifice."(Henry)

Abraham though incredibly wealthy introduces himself as a stranger and sojourner in a land his God planned to give his seed through the end of time. Abraham publicly lowered himself as he requests a place to bury his wife's body. In making himself humble before the local leaders, Abraham is recognized as a prince of God amongst those present. The Canaanites were willing to allow Abraham to place his dead amongst their own which was not a practice allowed by Jewish custom during their possession of the land. Abraham was given the choice of any sepulcher within the local burying ground.

The language employed in Genesis 23:6 by the "sons of Heth" residing in this place is telling. "Hear us, my lord: thou [art] a mighty prince among us: in the choice of our sepulchers bury thy dead; none of us shall withhold from thee his sepulcher, but that thou mayest bury thy dead." (KJV)

Hear, concerning this situation, listen with attention and interest, understand what we are saying, give heed to what we say and judge our words are all phrase that enhance the meaning of "Hear us." These "sons of Heath'" were emphatically making a point. The point is a little lost in the King James translation, "thou art a mighty prince among us." The significant word within this phrase is *Elohiym*.

The name Elohiym is first mentioned in Genesis 1.1. "In the beginning Elohiym created the heavens and the earth." These 'sons of Heth" had watched the life Abraham was living. Elohiym was written all over Abraham. When Abraham had a need and humbly asked for their assistance their response was profound. Abraham, they said, you are our master and we are your servants. You, Abraham, are lifted up among us as the chief, the prince, the leader for the Creator God. As a people we will withhold nothing from you, take what you will. The "sons of Heth" willing allowed their sacred burying ground to receive the remains of this stranger among them with God's light shining through him.

So Ephron the Hittite appears. Ephron is the first individual specifically identified as a Hittite in the Bible. Given the choice of any gravesite amongst these people, Abraham chooses, picks, elects the cave of Machpelah which is owned by Ephron. From the "sons of Heth" Abraham elects Ephron's property to be the repository of Sarah's earthly remains. And Abraham offers to purchase the property.

Matthew Henry shares in his commentary, "Those that have least of this earth find a grave in it. Abraham provided, not cities, as Cain and Nimrod, but a sepulcher, to be a constant memorandum of death to himself and his posterity, that he and they might learn to die daily. This sepulcher is said to be *at the end of the field*; for, whatever our possessions are, there is a sepulcher at the end of them. To be a token of his belief and expectation of the resurrection; for why should such care be taken of the body if it be thrown away forever, and must not rise again? Abraham, in this, said plainly that he sought a better country, that is, a heavenly. Abraham is content to be still flitting, while he lives, but secures a place where, when he dies his flesh may rest in hope." (Henry) And in all these actions Ephron the Hittite observed a "prince of God amongst men."

Ephron in turn generously gives the property to Abraham. This generous spirit, this act of kindness, displayed by Ephron is perhaps a spiritual characteristic passed on to generations of Hittites that follow. Ephron revealed a tenderness of heart that reached out to a grieving man at the death of his wife. He laid aside his interest in this possession and presented it as a gift to relieve the burden carried by Abraham in this time of loss. Ephron was not only making a sacrificial gift to Abraham, he was making it to the God Abraham represented.

Abraham was an incredibly wealthy man in comparison to Ephron, and though he greatly appreciates Ephron's kind offer he knows that purchasing the property at a fair market value will remove all doubt for posterity with who title to the property lies. As with any relationship with God such as this picture of Ephron's election, it is initiated by God. And the contractual relationship is sealed for eternity with a payment made by the Creator God.

Ephron the Hittite calls Abraham his brother and lowers himself and concedes to Abraham's wishes in the matter. Publicly Ephron the Hittite is immersed in 400 pieces of Abraham's silver. Ephron and Abraham are joined together in a contract conveying this property to Abraham forever. It is the only property Abraham will ever own in the land God promises to his heirs. Ephron's election and blessing for deeding over the rights and privileges he had as owner of this property to its proper owner Abraham will be revealed as God's work cascades through time.

Yet this was a motley crew surrounding Abraham as this funeral. The people were Canaanites, they were the "sons of Heth", but they were not all Hittites. As a group they have much the same ancestral lineage, and suffered under the same curses visited upon them by their ancestor's behavior. From whom did these people spawn?

In Genesis chapter ten the genealogy of these peoples are recorded. All peoples of the world were destroyed in the great flood save those on the ark with Noah. Noah had three sons, and they were named Shem, Ham and Japheth. These three sons were the progenitors of all who walk the earth today.

In Genesis 10.6 we find Noah's second son Ham had four sons, "And the sons of Ham; Cush, and Mizraim, and Phut, and Canaan. And as discovered earlier the Hittites were Canaanites, and Canaan was the fourth son of Ham.

In Gen 10:15-20 we find still more, "And Canaan begat Sidon his firstborn, and Heth, And the Jebusite, and the Amorite, and the Girgasite, And the Hivite, and the Arkite, and the Sinite, And the Arvadite, and the Zemarite, and the Hamathite: and afterward were the families of the Canaanites spread abroad. The border of the Canaanites was from Sidon, as thou comest to Gerar, unto Gaza; as thou goest, unto Sodom, and Gomorrah, and Admah, and Zeboim, even unto Lasha. These are the sons of Ham, after their families, after their tongues, in their countries, and in their nations."(KJV)

So to simplify Uriah the Hittite's was descended from Noah's second son named Ham. Ham had four sons, and the fourth son's name was Canaan. And Genesis twenty-five shares that the Hittites were descended from Heth, and Heth was Canaan's second son. So the heritage moves from Noah to Ham, from Ham to Canaan, from Canaan to Heth, and from Heth to the Hittites. It is also important to note that included in the boundaries of Canaanite descendants were the cities of Sodom and Gomorrah.

It is an amazing demonstration of God's grace that He would amongst all the wickedness of the Canaanites preserve a remnant. God's grace is not withheld from those who turn to the living God for mercy.

Uriah the Hittite was of course one of King David's mighty men on whom God's grace and mercy is bestowed. He was indeed a great soldier and warrior. Given the fact that language and family ties generally keep ancient clans fairly geographically fixed, Hebron, the burial ground of Abraham and Sarah, was the home of the Hittites. It was the general location where many of the individuals designated as King David's "mighty men" first joined him. Hebron was also Caleb's inheritance when the children of Israel finally returned to the promised.

So let us briefly revisit the Caleb, Hebron, Hittite connection. The Exodus has started and the Children of Israel have exited Egypt. The descendents of Abraham, Isaac and Jacob have experienced the plagues visited on the Egyptians. As a people the Hebrews experienced the death angel's Passover of Egypt that killed the first born of every Egyptian man, women and animal. Their eyes beheld the parting of the Red Sea and the destruction of Pharaoh's army. The three million person caravan arrives at Kadesh-barnea. Twelve spies are sent into the Promised Land to verify that all the wonders God promised are present.

The spies return with their reports. All the wonders God promised are there in the Promised Land for the taking, but the 10 of the twelve spies could not help notice just how big the bad guys were that lived in the Promised Land. The ten reported that they looked like grasshoppers in the eyes of the current residents. The inference was that upon entering the Promised Land they would be squashed like bugs by the giants that lived there.

Two of the spies, Joshua and Caleb, remembered the watery graves of the Egyptian charioteers. Caleb thought it was a no contest between the biggest and most intimidating giants in the land when he made his report to Moses. Caleb would enter into the fight with God on his side. These giants also lived on the best of the best land in the Promised Land. It just so happened to be Hebron where Abraham bought his burial ground from Ephron the Hittite. So the Hittites lived in an area identified by Caleb as the residence of the nastiest giants in the entire Promised Land. Uriah the Hittite dwelled on the land of Hebron. Caleb did receive Hebron as his inheritance upon entry to the Promised Land. For Caleb's faithfulness we will see in later chapters that his inheritance required no combat.

In summary there is biblical mention of Hittites resident in the land of Canaan. God through Abraham elected a Hittite who willingly submitted to God's desires through Abraham's requests. The Hittites living at and about Hebron possess the most fruitful land in all of the Promised Land. Caleb describes these Hittite people as the biggest of all giant warriors in the whole of the Promised Land. The consistency in the naming of names and places in God's word allows Bible readers to rightfully conclude that Uriah the Hittite was of the clan of Hittites that lived on or about Hebron and was descended from the Hittite stock that struck a deal with God through Abraham. A group of these Hittites recognizes the Promised Land belongs to the heirs of Abraham and willingly gives up their right to it. And Uriah the Hittite, in honor of the commitment made by his forefathers, swore allegiance to the rightful heir of Hebron because Uriah, the flame of Lord, recognized Elohiym's anointing on David as his forefather's recognized Elohiym's anointing on Abraham.

The Christian world is now focused on the spread of radical Islam. News outlets are biting their nails over stories on radical sects which are determined to wipe Israel and the church off the map. But do we understand that Christ wants these Muslims saved and that His grace can touch a remnant amongst these twisted hate driven souls? As Saul, the apostle Paul murdered early Christians. Paul's fervor for killing Christian's was no less zealous than those Muslims beheading Christian's in the Middle East today. Pray that the blind Muslim eyes are opened and Muslim ears hear Christ's call, "Why are you persecuting me."

Chapter Three

The Curse on the Hittites and did Uriah fulfill the curse?

As was discovered earlier Uriah the Hittite's is descended from Noah's second son named Ham. Ham had four sons, and the fourth son's name was Canaan. And Genesis twenty-five shares that the Hittites were descended from Heth, and Heth was Canaan's second son. So the heritage moves from Noah to Ham, from Ham to Canaan, from Canaan to Heth, and from Heth to the Hittites.

In Genesis chapter nine a series of events are recorded that have changed the course of history many times through the centuries. Previous chapters record Satan's continued hatred of God and Satan's efforts to corrupt all of mankind. Satan's attempts to stymie God's plan for the redemption of men ran rampant in the early centuries following Adam and Eve's ejection from the Garden of Eden. The race became so perverse that even after nearly a century of Noah's pounding and sawing not one man, women or child would hear God's voice calling them to enter into the ark to preserve life. Two of every kind of animal are sensitive enough to hear God's voice to enter into a brighter future, but not one single person yielded to God's call save the members of Noah's family.

The long predicted rains that had punctuated Noah's sermons for years started to fall. Thunder, lighting and the relentless pounding of huge raindrops destroyed dwellings that were never designed to withstand the effects of heavy weather. The fountains of the deep opened, and volcanic and seismic activity devastated the landscape. Within the safety of the ark God's hand of protection sustained eight souls, Noah and his wife, his three sons, and each of their wives. Every other man, women and child on the face of the earth died in this cataclysm.

After forty days and nights of the worst devastation the earth has ever witnessed, God stretched forth His hand and the destruction ceased and the restoration process began. Noah and his family disembark and start the process of being fruitful and multiplying upon the earth. Noah built an alter and sacrifice a burnt offering unto the Lord, Genesis 8.21-22 says "And the LORD smelled a sweet savor; and the LORD said in his heart, I will not again curse the ground any more for man's sake; for the imagination of man's heart [is] evil from his youth; neither will I again smite any more everything living, as I have done. While the earth remaineth, seedtime and harvest, and cold and heat, and summer and winter, and day and night shall not cease."(KJV)

God here acknowledges "the imagination of man's heart is evil from his youth." (KJV) The sin is born into him, and God takes pity on men. Redemption for men's sin will be resolved in a different fashion other than the forfeiture of a man's lives. The race is degenerate in every way, and no price a man could pay including the forfeiture of his own life will redeem him from that sinful nature.

So without fear of another catastrophe befalling the family Noah and his sons, Japheth, Shem and Ham, went about spreading over the earth and building a new future. But it did not take long for the evil imaginations of man's heart to resurface in the *tabula rasa* of this new world, and the trouble comes.

Genesis 9:22-29 says, "And Noah began to be an husbandman, and he planted a vineyard: And he drank of the wine, and was drunken; and he was uncovered within his tent. And Ham, the father of Canaan, saw the nakedness of his father, and told his two brethren without. And Shem and Japheth took a garment, and laid it upon both their shoulders, and went backward, and covered the nakedness of their father; and their faces were backward, and they saw not their father's nakedness. And Noah awoke from his wine, and knew what his younger son had done unto him. And he said, Cursed be Canaan; a servant of servants shall he be unto his brethren. And he said, Blessed be the LORD God of Shem; and Canaan shall be his servant. God shall enlarge Japheth, and he shall dwell in the tents of Shem; and Canaan shall be his servant." (KJV)

So following the flood Noah decides to plant a vineyard and ferment for himself wine. Readers are not told where this taste for strong drink was planted in Noah's mind. Perhaps it was a remembrance that he carried with him from the days of hard labor before the flood. Perhaps he had tasted of the grape during his own youth. Whatever the reason for the decision to harvest the fruit of the vine and process the grapes into fermented wine, it indeed was the course Noah set for himself.

Noah's actions set the stage for a terrible turn of events. Noah drank his wine to the point of intoxication. Noah continued to consume the wine to the point he passed out in his tent, but somewhere during the binge and prior to his passing out Noah managed to shed all his clothing. The language used suggests that Noah was shamefully exposed. During this period while his father Noah lay unconscious and naked within his tent, Ham entered and something terrible took place.

When Noah awoke from his drunkenness Genesis 9:24 says that Noah "knew what his younger son had done unto him." (KJV) So the action taken by Ham in the tent seems to be immediately known to Noah. Shaking off the cob webs of his hang-over Noah clearly perceived that his youngest son Ham had performed some act that was readily identifiable as his handiwork. There was no process of elimination, there was no investigation, but there was a father who knew the proclivities of his sons. There was no doubt in the mind of this father that the act perpetrated against him in his unconscious state was the work of Ham.

The horrible actions taken by Ham against his father are hidden in the words used to describe the events. There have been numerous speculations as to the nature of Ham's sin. Some have argued that Noah was castrated, so the inheritance left to his three sons would not be further diluted. Still others have argued that Ham raped his own mother during his father's stupor, and Canaan was the spurious offspring of that incestuous union. Yet other sources suggest that Ham raped his own father satisfying his own lusts while Noah's drunkenness would not allow any resistance. Still others suggest that the act of merely looking upon his father's nakedness and speaking about the event was his sin, but this scenario of "looking" does not adequately explain the actionable work or labor that produces a direct effect suggested by the verb translated as "had done unto him". Hearing someone talking about an action is significantly different from first hand knowing the effect of an act.

The sins of a father are often visited upon his offspring and in this case the punishment. It is important to note that included in the boundaries of Canaanite descendants were the cities of

Sodom and Gomorrah. Noah's judgment in the form of a dreadful curse fell not only upon Ham but also Ham's son. Through the inspiration of the Holy Spirit the curse fell upon Noah's grandson, Canaan. God alone can know the content of a man's heart, and God alone knows the future. Canaan and all the generations that would spring from his loins would carry a curse and obligation. Genesis 9:25 relates the curse, "And he said, Cursed be Canaan; a servant of servants shall he be unto his brethren."(KJV)

Throughout history the descendants of Ham have struggled against the bonds of servitude to which they were cursed. A wicked and rebellious demonic spirit encourages Ham's descendants to fight against the judgment placed upon them. Rather than submitting to the roll of servant of servants, rather than be slaves to their brothers, Ham's descendants have pressed dominion over his brothers' descendents rather than their willing servitude.

The sons of Ham are listed in Genesis 10:6 as Cush, Mizraim, Phut and Canaan. Mizraim's decedents became the Pharaohs of Egypt. Mizraim forced God's chosen people into four hundred years of backbreaking labor and slavery. God's judgment was displayed against Mizraim when through their continued resistance to subjugating themselves and letting their masters depart in peace suffered the dreadful plagues of Egypt.

From the loins of Cush sprang the likes of Nimrod whose satanic nature was never more evident than in his affront to God. Nimrod thought he could confront God face to face through the building of a Tower of Babel. Nimrod would reach up into the sky and pull God back down to men. His futile efforts building the Tower of Babel brought God's judgment through the introduction of hundreds of languages into the minds of men which in turn dispersed people throughout the world. His name means hunter, but he was a hunter not of game animals but of men. Nimrod was a hunter in the sense that Hitler was a hunter who tracked down God's people and sought to destroy them.

Phut is the most mysterious of Ham's sons. Research and biblical references place these descendants of Ham in the area of Yemen and Somalia. Biblical references would suggest a warlike people. Are current residents of these lands, who today continue practicing anti-Semitic blood lust, rooted in the ancient Hamitic curse?

Uriah the Hittite was subject to this Canaanite curse. Uriah the Hittite was to perform as a servant of a servant for a descendant of Japheth or to a descendant of Shem. It was the plan written for his life by the Holy Spirit. To be aligned with God's purpose for his life and his redemption Uriah was destined for a role of servitude to descendants of his ancient uncles to remain in right standing with God. Is it a cursing or blessing to have the life of being a servant's servant? Uriah remained last in line with little earthly recognition when the kudos of this world are passed out. Yet when the rolls are opened up yonder and Christ's rewards revealed the last shall be first and the first shall be last.

Chapter Four

Uriah the Hittite is a dead man walking.

Uriah the Hittite was a dead man walking. As learned earlier The Hittites were one of the family groups descended from Canaan that occupied a portion of the land God had promised to the descendants of Abraham. Squatters rarely will depart from land they have occupied for generations without a fight. Whether or not they have a legal right to the property, they claim it and see it as their own.

These Canaanites inherited the rebellious natures of their forefathers. As a collection of small kingdoms these peoples were not about to yield to the curse placed on them centuries before and become the servant of servants to the Israelites. The Canaanites heard the Israelites were on the march and that God had held back the flooding waters of the Jordan River. Upon hearing that the Israelites had crossed the Jordan on dry ground the Canaanite minds harkened back to the terror that first gripped them when the story of the army of Pharaoh being swallowed up by the Red Sea first entered their psyche when nomadic merchants shared the news flash and incredible gossip as they traveled through Canaan. The Canaanite hearts melted within them and the starch in their shorts was lost forever. The Canaanites knew that their fate was sealed, and they were doomed. But God hardened their hearts, and they would not yield just as their distant cousins in Egypt failed to yield. The Canaanites would fight the rightful possession of the land to their death.

Spiritually the children of Israel had changed their destination when the passed through the symbolic baptism of the Red Sea. They were a born again people, but they carried the baggage of Egypt with them in the heads and hearts. The chosen people had lived as servants for so long in Egypt that their thoughts were Egyptian thoughts. When times got rough in the desert their thoughts traveled back to the leeks and cucumbers of Egypt, to golden gods of their captors, and to a life with no demands from God.

The Israelites thought a return to servitude in Egypt was preferable to the Promised Land where God demanded an act of faith. At Kadish-barnea these chosen people balked at the responsibility that the born again experience carries with it. They clutched to the carnal sin imbedded in their hearts and inculcated by several centuries of human experience.

The chosen people had become comfortable in the role of being a servant to Egypt, and they initially rebelled against the personal responsibility that comes with the cross and the resurrected nature when first confronted with the challenges of crossing the Jordan. Luke 17:33 says "Whosoever shall seek to save his life shall lose it; and whosoever shall lose his life shall preserve it." (KJV) And so a generation of Israelites perished in the desert never knowing the blessings of the Promised Land and a life controlled by Christ.

After forty years in the desert the business of death was a daily experience. Given Biblical estimates that 600,000 men with their wives and children started the Exodus with Moses, it is easily concluded that at least 1.2 million fathers and mothers died during this period. Considering a fairly even distribution of death during the wanderings, funerals services were a daily event for friends and family. The death of 1.2 million people over 40 years would require funerals at a rate of 80 to 100 per day.

With the placement of the last gravestone a new generation of chosen people had grown up and taken their place in tribal leadership. It is again time to put the question to the nation; it is time to take possession of the milk and honey of the Promised Land. And taking possession of the land God demands a change in occupation. This generation entering this Promised Land laid aside the shovels used in burying their own dead and pick up the warriors sword as they entered a land where no quarter was to be given and no prisoners were to be taken. Every man, women, child and baby living in Canaan is to be put to the sword.

So Uriah was a Hittite. What were God's plans for the Hittites who dwelled in the land of Canaan? What was the Israelite's charge to faithfully follow God's direction in their conquest of the Promised Land? In Exodus 34.10-14 we find the initial marching orders issued through Moses saying, "And he said, Behold, I make a covenant: before all thy people I will do marvels, such as have not been done in all the earth, nor in any nation: and all the people among which thou [art] shall see the work of the LORD: for it [is] a terrible thing that I will do with thee. Observe thou that which I command thee this day: behold, I drive out before thee the Amorite, and the Canaanite, and the Hittite, and the Perizzite, and the Hivite, and the Jebusite. Take heed to thyself, lest thou make a covenant with the inhabitants of the land whither thou goest, lest it be for a snare in the midst of thee: But ye shall destroy their altars, break their images, and cut down their groves: For thou shalt worship no other god: for the LORD, whose name is Jealous, is a jealous God..." (KJV)

Gods intentions for the residents of Canaan were again stated in Joshua 3:10. "And Joshua said, Hereby ye shall know that the living God is among you, and that he will without fail drive out from before you the Canaanites, and the Hittites, and the Hivites, and the Perizzites, and the Girgashites, and the Amorites, and the Jebusites." (KJV)

The usurpers, the squatters were to be completely driven out and eradicated from the land. The rebellious descendants of Ham, Canaan and Shem were a scourge on the land. The deviant religions practiced by these interlopers were a stench in the nostrils of God. There was to be nothing remaining in the land of these cursed descendants of Ham. The perverse sexual nature of their religious practice was not to remain. No memorial, no trinket, no idol and no memory of these people were to remain in the land to infect God's newly circumcised people.

God had given the cities and land and all that was within it to children of Israel. God charged them with the responsibility of taking possession of the gift. God wanted His chosen people and their land to be totally dedicated to His worship, so there were conditions on how the people were to be conquered and how the people were to take possession of the land. God did not want his people polluted by the descendants of Ham whose faithless hearts indulged in rebellious religious practices. Every man, women and child who stood in their path was to die.

Even the baby children? What possible harm could come from an innocent baby? Well babies grow up and become adult enemies. There is no quarter to be given even the most innocent affront to Almighty God. Sin is sin and it must be expunged. It is much like that small grudge we form when an affront goes unforgiven. We nurture that baby sin each time we see the person who perpetrated the hurt. Soon the small black spot on the soul manifests itself as a snarky comment to a spouse or friend regarding the character of the unforgiven. The virus multiples and strengthens through further acts of gossip that strangely seem to flow from lips unchallenged by good conscious. The baby and seemingly innocent little sin first harbored in our heart will inevitably grown up to be a killer. That is the reason all sin must die.

So the new generation passes before the stopped up waters of the Jordan River and into the Promised Land. Joshua orders a memorial built from twelve stones, taken by each of the twelve tribes from the middle of the Jordan River. A memorial stands in remembrance of a great event in a nation's history. Memorials help a people hold steady to the course established by their forefathers for their nation. The memorial stands to bring a people in heart, mind and faith back to a crossroads in their history. And is it is with all memorials, mementoes and keepsakes in our lives. We wear memorials on our wrist as jewelry. The charms worn by mothers commemorating the birth of her children and grandchildren, or a gold wrist watch commemorating the years of dedicated service to an employer. Walls and mantels house the recordings of significant events as photographs, plaques or trophies that commemorate our highest of high moments. Graduations, promotions, weddings, and births adorn the home and office as pictures of frozen moments in time that changed our lives.

The first battle in the campaign was at Jericho. God's desires were faithfully followed and all within the walled city died save one family. Rahab the harlot and those in her house were the one exception. God commanded, "Only Rahab the harlot shall live, she and that entire are with her in the house, because she hid the messengers that we sent." (KJV) In Joshua 6.21 we are told, "And they utterly destroyed all that was in the city, both man and woman, young and old, and ox, and sheep, and ass, with the edge of the sword." (KJV)

So the conquest proceeds as God dictated save a small difficulty in battle for the next city named Ai. As is often the case in the world today, men and women are drawn to sin through the sirens call of fine clothes and money. A fellow named Achen acts deceitfully and takes from Jericho items that God has forbidden. Shamefully men often try to hide their sin and choose to believe that indulgence in sin has no impact on anyone but themselves. The deceit Achen perpetrated at Jericho costs the lives of 27 fellow Israelites none of whom Achen may have had a personal relationship. As is always the case, lies and deceits are Satan's method of keeping a foothold in that area of our heart God desires to clean.

The next kingdom to be conquered was the inhabitants of Gibeon. Gibeon was a collection of cities as described in Joshua 9.17. "And the children of Israel journeyed, and came unto their cities on the third day. Now their cities [were] Gibeon, and Chephirah, and Beeroth, and Kirjathjearim." (KJV) The people dwelling in these cities are recognized as Hivites. The name Hivite is a geographic designation, so it is a reference to the group of people living in this geographic area. The interesting twist is many Bible scholars believe the Hivites to be a sub-group of the Hittites. So it is in a sense safe to say that all Hivites are Hittites, but not all Hittites are Hivites. It would be akin to saying all Virginians are Americans, but not all

Americans are Virginians save the fact that these were a relatively homogeneous people groups. Blending of these people groups did occur as is the case in modern America. Italian-American, African-American, Native American, Asian American have all melded into the fabric of the United States.

It also seems these communities acted collectively as a republic rather than being ruled by a monarch. And collectively a decision was made to contact the Israelites prior to their arrival and military conquest. It seems these four communities all decided that the Almighty God traveling with Israel was the one true God and that military action was completely fruitless, so prior to armed conflict the Gibeonites decided to embrace the only course that provided a true hope of survival.

So Gibeon sent ambassadors to negotiate a league or treaty with Israel in an effort to insure their survival. The Gibeonite negotiating strategy was based on a rouse, but its foundation appears to be genuine. In Joshua 9.4 the Gibeonites are said to have acted "wilily'. Wilily is not an often used word in the Old Testament and is elsewhere translated as "prudence". Proverbs 1.4 says, "I wisdom dwell with prudence." (KJV) So the negotiating strategy is played out in Joshua 9.11 when the costumed Gibeonite ambassadors say, "Wherefore our elders and all the inhabitants of our country spake to us, saying, Take victuals with you for the journey, and go to meet them, and say unto them, We are your servants: therefore now make ye a league with us."(KJV)

How many times have unchurched folks entered the front door of God's house and said stupid stuff. Worldly people often think they have to somehow cut a deal with God, and God will generally just chuckle. The crucial matter to be considered is the Gibeonites heard the call of God and arrived at God's doorstep to humble themselves.

God is the only one who truly knows a people's heart and whether the profession coming from the mouths of the Gibeonites truly reflected the content of their hearts. The confession was, "We are your servants." The word servant also could be translated slave. Think of how the many times the New Testament apostles call themselves "slaves of Christ."

Recall from chapter two the line from whom the Gibeonites descended. Noah's second son was named Ham. Ham had four sons, and the fourth son's name was Canaan. Genesis twenty-five shares that the Hittites were descended from Heth, and Heth was Canaan's second son. So the heritage moves from Noah to Ham, from Ham to Canaan, from Canaan to Heth, and from Heth to the Hittites. Gibeonites were a sub-group of Hittites know as Hivites. The Gibeonites were cursed with Noah's curse that they were to be the servant of servants to their Israelite cousins. The Gibeon confession was, "We are your servants." The Gibeonite rouse was discovered but it was of little matter for the heart was right and the confession true. If the Gibeonite collective heart was not pure and repentant, they would have never been able to utter the confession. Such a confession would have stuck in the throats of a Canaanite descendent were the heart unrepentant, ask Pharaoh. The Gibeonites readily accepted the "servant of servants" role in which they will carry water and chop wood.

God honored the Gibeonite confession. Rather than allowing the Gibeonites to be abused in their servitude by the general Israelite population, God took them home to His house. Joshua 9:27

shares, "And Joshua made them (the Gibeonites) that day hewers of wood and drawers of water for the congregation, and for the altar of the LORD, even unto this day, in the place which he should choose." (KJV)

When the Psalms were written by David we truly discover the blessing God poured out on these gentile Gibeonite people because of their confession and willingness to assume a role of servitude in the new kingdom He was building. Psalm 84:10-11 sings, "For a day in thy courts is better than a thousand. I had rather be a doorkeeper in the house of my God, than to dwell in the tents of wickedness. For the LORD God is a sun and shield: the LORD will give grace and glory: no good thin] will he withhold from them that walk uprightly." (KJV)

Lest, the naysayer suggest this scenario is all a concoction of the writer's imagination, remember Rahab's confession and salvation. The walls of an entire city disintegrated save her house, and she walked out unscathed. So what validation is found in the Gibeonite confession? Let us read the story:

Joshua 10:1-10 says "Now it came to pass, when Adonizedek king of Jerusalem had heard how Joshua had taken Ai, and had utterly destroyed it; as he had done to Jericho and her king, so he had done to Ai and her king; and how the inhabitants of Gibeon had made peace with Israel, and were among them; That they feared greatly, because Gibeon [was] a great city, as one of the royal cities, and because it [was] greater than Ai, and all the men thereof [were] mighty. Wherefore Adonizedek king of Jerusalem sent unto Hoham king of Hebron, and unto Piram king of Jarmuth, and unto Japhia king of Lachish, and unto Debir king of Eglon, saying, Come up unto me, and help me, that we may smite Gibeon: for it hath made peace with Joshua and with the children of Israel. Therefore the five kings of the Amorites, the king of Jerusalem, the king of Hebron, the king of Jarmuth, the king of Lachish, the king of Eglon, gathered themselves together, and went up, they and all their hosts, and encamped before Gibeon, and made war against it. And the men of Gibeon sent unto Joshua to the camp to Gilgal, saying, Slack not thy hand from thy servants; come up to us quickly, and save us, and help us: for all the kings of the Amorites that dwell in the mountains are gathered together against us. So Joshua ascended from Gilgal, he, and all the people of war with him, and all the mighty men of valour. And the LORD said unto Joshua, Fear them not: for I have delivered them into thine hand; there shall not a man of them stand before thee." (KJV)

So the surrounding Canaanite kings get pissed off because of the Gibeonite submission. These Kings are pissed because the Gibeonites no longer insulate them from the coming onslaught. These Kings are pissed because they think the Gibeonites are a very bad example to other Canaanites. These Kings are pissed because the Gibeonites yield up their powerless false gods and idols to the One True God. How many times do we see the old way of life haunt us as new Christians? The old life comes back telling us lies and seeking to destroy our new found covenant. But what answer did the Gibeonites give? They called out to God through Joshua for help. It was the correct course of action.

God tells Joshua the only words he needs to hear, "Fear them not: for I have delivered them into thane hand; there shall not a man of them stand before thee." God delivered them? This entire series of events was God's plan to deliver the unrepentant haters to their judgment. Wow, and what an exclamation point God chooses to use!

Joshua 10.10 says, "And the LORD discomfited them before Israel, and slew them with a great slaughter at Gibeon, and chased them along the way that goeth up to Bethhoron, and smote them to Azekah, and unto Makkedah. And it came to pass, as they fled from before Israel, [and] were in the going down to Bethhoron, that the LORD cast down great stones from heaven upon them unto Azekah, and they died: [they were] more which died with hailstones than [they] whom the children of Israel slew with the sword." (KJV)

What has just happened?

A huge NATO like army shows up to slaughter the Gibeonites for their return to a truly godlike lifestyle. Joshua meets these Canaanites on the field of battle, and they become so confused they are powerless to defend themselves and the slaughter is on. Joshua's army cannot seem to kill the Canaanites fast enough with the sword, and well over half of this confederated army starts running from the field in full and without order retreat.

And then suddenly, God. How do men know when God does a "then suddenly"? Men just cannot run far enough or fast enough to escape a "then suddenly." Joshua's army looks up from their hand to hand combat to a tremendous noise as the ground beneath their feet begins to shake. The sight Joshua's army sees in front of them causes their jaws drop and knees buckle with wonder and awe at the power of Almighty God. It was a sight no man had ever seen, yet it is a sight men will once again witness as God will again use the weapon he employed this day during the end of days.

John the Revelator speaks of it in Revelation 16.21, "And there fell upon men a great hail out of heaven, [every stone] about the weight of a talent: and men blasphemed God because of the plague of the hail; for the plague thereof was exceeding great." (KJV)

God uses hailstones to destroy these armies. When God uses hailstones these are no ordinary hailstones. These soldiers did not die from being pelted to death with pea gravel size hailstones. When God uses blocks of ice from heaven to kill you, there is no doubt you are dead when it hits you. John notes the weight of these hailstones. The hailstones weighed a talent each. In the ancient weighs and measure a talent varied whether it was speaking of gold or silver, but it is safe to say that these hailstones weighted between 75 and 95 pounds each.

A ninety pound hailstone would be the size of a huge beach ball. This aerodynamic beauty would fall from the sky faster than a top fuel dragster does a quarter mile. Imagine a 90 pound ball of ice falling from the sky at a terminal velocity in excess of three hundred miles per hour! Remember the last time a twenty pound bag of ice was dropped on the kitchen floor to make the cubes useable. Recall the noise it made when you dropped the bag those three short feet to the floor?

Well, after the first 300 mph 90 pound hailstone gouged a giant hole in the earth Joshua's army no longer needed imagination. When those ice missiles impacted a fleeing soldier's body it most likely exploded from the impact. I don't think using the term splat can even come close to describing what Joshua's soldiers witnessed that day. The bodies of the slain enemy soldiers were relentless pulverized by hailstone after hailstone.

There was no doubt amongst Joshua's army who had won the day. "Then suddenly" won the day.

The tons of ice slowly melt washing the battle field clean of the blood. The rivers ran red with the battlefield run off. No Canaanite ran fast enough or far enough to escape. Only in the battles found in the Book of Revelation will the soldiers find the time to blaspheme God during a hailstone attack. Inside armored vehicles as the pile driving impact of these hailstones slowly pancake the armor shell will soldiers being slowly hammered to death inside their modern marvels have a few moments to relish the cold, damn God, and enter an eternity of burning flames haunted with the desire to experience the cold of those hailstones one last time.

As for the Hittite people in southern Palestine living outside Gibeon, all are recorded as destroyed. Archeology indicates Hittite people existed outside the boundaries of the Promised Land, but it makes little sense to think a Hittite would willing migrate to a country where a death warrant is sworn out for all of his or her nationality. It makes much more sense to believe Uriah the Hittite's progenitors survived the cleansing of Canaanites from the Promised Land amongst the Gibeonite Hivite Hittite people who surrendered as servants. Quite possibly these Gibeonites were descendants of Ephron the Hittite whose confession of faith in Elohiym through his offerings of a burial ground to Abraham established an eternal connection between Abraham and Ephron. Is it also too much to believe God honored and sustained the covenant and blessing on Ephron the Hittite's heritage as He did with Abraham's heritage?

Chapter 5

A change in name for his people.

Names carry significant meaning in God's word, and when a name for a person or people changes it is a significant event.

Noah was ten generations removed from the first man into whom God breathed life. Noah's name means rest. Noah's second son was named Ham, and Ham is from whom the Hittite linage descends.

Ham is the son of Noah who defiles Noah in some fashion while Noah is drunk and naked in his tent. The name Ham translates to mean warm or hot.

Ham's son Canaan is the next name in the line of Uriah the Hittite's ancestors. Canaan was the recipient of the curse Noah placed on Ham. Canaan's name according to Strong's Exhaustive Concordance means to be humble, be humbled, be subdued, and to be brought down, be low, be under, and be brought into subjection. (Strong) This name wholly describes what the eventual end is for all of Canaan's descendants.

Genesis twenty-five shares that the Hittites were descended from Heth, and Heth was Canaan's second son. Heth's name is understood to mean terror or fear. In Joshua 1.4 the name is applied to the kings of Canaan or the land of the sons of terror.

The name Hittite literally means "the sons of Heth." So the heritage moves from Noah to Ham, from "rest" to "hot". As we move from Ham to Canaan the "hot" moves to "needs to be subdued." So the "hot" of Ham escalates in Canaan to a point where Canaan's pursuit of darkness "needs to be subdued".

From Canaan to Heth the escalation in evil continues with Heth. The meaning of Heth's name is "fear and terror". The Hittites are the "sons of Heth", or the "sons of fear and terror". It appears that by the time the Hittites appear in this family linage, the line is rotten to the core. Every son begat of Heth appears to be a terror.

But a proverb is about to be turned on its head. God can plant his goodness in the heart of any man and create life where only death remains. One bad apple in the form of Ham has spoiled the entire barrel of apples, but with God there is always a remnant.

"And he said unto me, Son of man, can these bones live? and I answered, O Lord God, thou knowest." Ezekiel 37:3 (KJV)

The spiritually embers that founded the United States had all but subsided in the decades following the American Revolution. Amongst the hearts a few New England pastors the desire for revival stirred. A young man named Edward Dorn Griffin ministering a small church in New Hartford, Connecticut penned a sermon entitled <u>Can These Bones Live?</u> which is one of the matches that ignite the fire of America's Second Great Awakening. Griffin's sermon shares:

"This valley of bones represented the whole house of Israel in Babylon, dead to all hope, and most of them dead in sin; whom God intended to raise to holiness and restore to the land of their fathers, and to whom he directed the vision to be thus explained: "Ye shall know that I am the Lord when I have opened your graves,—and shall put my Spirit in you, and ye shall live, and I shall place you in your own land." Placing them in their own land, was only setting them up in the world after they were made alive; their resurrection consisted in rising from the death of sin by the power of the Holy Spirit. The vision therefore illustrates the natural condition of men in general, "dead in trespasses and sins" and cut off from hope, and their resurrection to spiritual life by the power of God.

Methinks I am standing today on the margin of a valley full of dry bones, —the bones of my kindred, at whose death my tears have often flowed. As I bend over the remains of those dear to me and mourn the wide desolation, I perceive the bones to be very dry. I see them disjointed and scattered through the valley in ruinous disorder. While I stand fixed in grief, a whisper comes from heaven, "Son of man, can these bones live?" I start at the joyous sound. I look at the valley again. To the eye of reason such an event seems impossible. The whisper swells upon my ear, "Son of man, can these bones live?" Agitated with hope and fear, and certain on whom the event depends, what can I answer but, "O Lord God, thou knowest"?" (Sprague, 1839)

As Griffin looked out on the cold lost hearts dwelling around him in colonial New England, let our hearts look back on the anguish in the Lord's heart over the lost state of the Hittite people. Sons of terror, the lot of them rotten to the core, dead in trespasses and sin, cut off from hope, and then the whisper comes, "Son of man, can these bones live?"

The evil that burned "hot" in Ham remained unchecked in his son "needs to be subdued". The evil that grew in Canaan was not subdued. Canaan's sin is visited on his son Heth who is a real "terror" and generates "fear" wherever he goes. And Heth's terror is visited on his children, and Heth's descendants are all terrorizing fear mongers.

This brings us to Abraham. Before Abraham, the father of multitudes, sets out on his journey to Canaan God knows the time He has appointed for Sarah's death. God knows the very spot He desires to have Sarah buried, and He leads Abraham to that spot. It is not that the cave in the ground at the town of Kirjatharba where Sarah is interred was particularly special. The Living God is a God of relationships. God through Abraham wants to create a remnant amongst the 'sons of terror.' God knows the heart that He had established in Ephron the Hittite. At Sarah's funeral an evangelistic sermon is preached, and Ephron the Hittite responds. Ephron the Hittite acknowledges and confesses Abraham's God when calling Abraham a "prince of God amongst men."

Only God can change a man's heart. A Hittite son of terror trained from youth to take anything he wanted through fear and intimidation offers to give Abraham the plot of ground to bury his wife. Giving, coming from a Hittite who from his very birth is nurtured and raised to take? Who changes the spots on this Hittite leopard? God alone can make these dry bones live again. God turns Ephron's heart as a child, and it was evident for all to see in the name Ephron carried.

His name, Ephron, may have made him a laughing stock amongst the Hittite people. One can only speculate the degree of chiding Ephron endured as he grew up in a Hittite culture that prized an in your face winner take all attitude. Ephron may at times have thought himself maligned for his name is not prized in a culture based on terror. Ephron's most unseemly name came from the heart God put in him. Ephron the Hittite translates to "fawn-like son of terror."

Mat 20:16 shares, "So the last shall be first, and the first last: for many be called, but few chosen." Amongst the Hittites "fawn-like" falls far short of terror. Ephron is the last chosen for the Hittite "roaring" team. All born again Christians should be thankful for God placing in us a heart that hears and responds to God's choosing and not to the roars of this world.

And so the name changes continue through God's Word. Abram gets a name changed to Abraham, Jacob gets a name change to Israel, Simon gets a make-over to Peter and Saul is christened Paul with his new birth.

So it is with these Hittites living in the city of Gibeon. These decedents of the "sons of terror" become the servants of the Levite servants in God's House. These Gibeonites descend from Epron's fawn-like heart. The spiritual heritage with which God has blessed these sons of Heth now enables this people to reside as carriers of wood and water in the House of God. No better job could be found for these people. Psalm 42.1 says, "As the hart panteth after the water brooks, so panteth my soul after thee, O God." (KJV) The "fawn-like" heart fetches water in the Temple.

So Gibeonite sons of terror have their name changed. The takers have become givers. These new givers are given a new name. The Gibeonite Hittites become the Nethinims. This born-again name God gives these Gibeonite Hittites is Nethinims which translates to "the given". (Strong) A group of people with fawn like hearts that God gives to Himself to joyfully carry water in His house. The Nethinims are a people who actually believe Psalm 84:10, "For a day in thy courts is better than a thousand. I had rather be a doorkeeper in the house of my God, than to dwell in the tents of wickedness." (KJV)

As Christians do we should find ourselves always content with the position God has given us to fulfill? In Philippians 4:11-13 Christians are charged to, "Not that I speak in respect of want: for I have learned, in whatsoever state I am, therewith to be content. I know both how to be abased, and I know how to abound: everywhere and in all things I am instructed both to be full and to be hungry, both to abound and to suffer need. I can do all things through Christ which strengtheneth me." (KJV) So if chopping wood and carrying buckets of water seems like the mundane task in which as a Christian you find yourself, then choose to immerse yourself in the task with the passion of a fawn-like heart drinking from the cold refreshing crystal clear waters of a rushing mountain stream.

Chapter 6

How do you grow up to become one of David's mighty men?

Uriah the Hittite first appears amid David's time of trial with King Saul. David is anointed to become King of Israel by the greatest religious leader and prophet of his day, Samuel. Samuel held great influence in the land given his special relationship with God. There exists significant circumstantial evidence that Samuel may very well have touched Uriah the Hittite's life while he was young.

Everyone in the Israel was aware of Samuel's story. His mother Hanna had been barren for years. Hanna cries out to God to make her womb fruitful, and she promises to consecrate her first born to God. God answers Hanna's prayer with the birth of a son who is named Samuel. When Samuel is of age Hanna presents him to Eli the High Priest for Temple for the vow of the Nazarite as she had promised God.

But much turmoil exists in the land at that time. Only a single generation had been born into the Promised Land after the passing of the Joshua and Caleb generation. Yet in this short time God's chosen people have turned their back on Him.

Judges 2:8-10 shares, "And Joshua the son of Nun, the servant of the LORD, died, being an hundred and ten years old. And they buried him in the border of his inheritance in Timnathheres, in the mount of Ephraim, on the north side of the hill Gaash. And also all that generation were gathered unto their fathers: and there arose another generation after them, which knew not the LORD, nor yet the works which he had done for Israel." (KJV)

Joshua enters the Promised Land at an age of 80 years, and he died at 110 years old. So a mere 30 years after entry into the

Promised Land all the children of Israel who were of the generation that enter with Joshua and Caleb were dead. And the "new generation" spoiled in the prosperity of the Promised Land and dulled by Baal worship's pervasive sexual promiscuity fell away from the God of Israel and knew not the Lord. The memorials built to honor God are left unkempt. The works which God had done for Israel are forgotten. So the dead parents in their enjoyment of the economic prosperity and their indulgence in pervasive sexual perversity found in the Promised Land utterly failed to bring up their children in the way that they should go. When these children are mature they know nothing of the mighty works of God. This generation is taught little to nothing of the recent past, and probably thought the stone monument at the site of the Jordan crossing little more than a pile of stones.

The children of Israel are enticed by the Canaanite religions which their parents had failed to completely eradicate from their land. The indulgence in the sordid sexual activities of the Canaanite religions sweeps through the land. Sex could be found in the nearest patch of trees as the goddesses of the groves plied their wares as do mini-skirted hookers on today's big city street corners. Fertility worship produces unwanted pregnancies, but the results of the sin cannot be covered in the secrecy of the confines of an abortion clinic as it is done in an America that turns away from God. Baal worship practices infant human sacrifice to resolve issues of unwanted pregnancies. Carry the newborn over to Baal, do a little heathen worship and walk away from a dead child sacrificed out of convenience with a conscience scrubbed clean through the practice of religion.

In the case of such rampant sexual intercourse the innocent born and unborn children seem to be the ones getting dead. In current culture the name of the unborn child has been changed to fetus to protect the guilty. Fetus, the name given millions of murdered unborn children, is the name change that has been executed to protect the reproductive rights, the choice and the sexual promiscuity of our current culture's goddess of the groves.

Through their moral and spiritual weakness Israel's enemies recognizes an opportunity. These neighboring enemies start to exploit the internal decay. The Philistines, a group of Canaanites living primarily to the southwest of the Promised Land, start sending raiding parties to steal, kill and destroy the people and fruit of the Promised Land. The Philistine's steal and occupy the lands given Israel by God. Today Israel is attacked from the southwest by Hamas who desires to steal and occupy the Promised Land. These Philistine affronts finally get this generation of Israel's dander up, so Israel goes to war. Thousands die in a humiliating defeat, but little else can be expected when they fail to put on the armor of God. But more humiliating still is the Ark of God is captured by the Philistines. Israel is defeated and the cry of a dying mother naming her son Ichabod, meaning the glory of God has departed, reverberated through the land. Though the children of Israel through there disobedience and ignorance lived outside God's protection, their God certainly had not lost His power or willingness to display it.

The celebration of the Philistine god's victory over the Holy God of Israel is short lived. The first day the Philistines set the Ark in their temple next to their god Dagon. The next morning Dagon was face down in the dirt. The Philistines pull Dagon back up. The second morning this huge stone statue is again face down in the dirt, but the excuse that it might be the result of an earthquake or a man made efforts is removed.

Dagon was a mermaid type of image. A human like head and hands were incorporated into a fish like body. The second morning Dagon is not only face down in the dirt before the Ark, but his head and the palms of his hands are cut off and only a fishy stump remains of Dagon. This huge idol took many hundreds of man hours to fashion from most likely stone, and yet here Dagon lies in the dust with his head and palms cut off. The head and palms did not separate from the stump due to breakage from being toppled over, but the stone was severed. This piece of stone had been cut through as a butter knife through warm butter. The cutting performed on the statue of Dagon was so unbelievably terrifying not only was Dagon prostrate before the ark, but the severed portions were placed on the threshold or podium on which Dagon stood. After seeing the sliced up stone no Philistine, not one of them, ever touched the threshold of that temple again. But Almighty God is not through with the Philistines.

As the plagues of Egypt specifically confronted each of Egypt's major gods, so it was to be with the Philistines. Dagon is fallen but the Philistines have not yet yielded, so God continued. A culture that practices the most deviant of sexually behaviors is struck down by Almighty God right where the Philistines like to practice their faith. Every man, big and small, young and old, is smitten by a grievous case of emerods. Emerods were nasty tumors visited on the genitalia and anus causing excruciating pain and the issuance of blood.

What a sense of humor and incredible judgment Almighty God delivers on these sexually deviant Philistines. Smitten with a dreadful disease that directly impacts the Philistines' lustful desire and the practice of their deviant religion, the Philistines call out for healing, but implementation of their faith means employment of the body parts smitten with painful tumors. So the Philistines do the next best. These idol makers make more worthless idols. The Philistines make gold images of their emerods. Say what? That's right; the Philistine's made little gold images of the tumors on their private parts.

Not unlike the plague of darkness God visited on Egypt where Yahweh makes impotent Egypt's main deity Ra, the sun god. Ra totally disappears and not even a torch would light for the

Egyptians. The only light that shined was inside the homes of the Hebrew children. What a wonderful picture of the indwelling Holy Spirit in a Christian's life today.

Finally, the plagues overcome the Philistine stubbornness. They return to Israel the Ark of God which is placed on a cart and sent back to Israel. The children of Israel had not been taught the God given instruction on how to care for the Holy Objects. When the Ark returns the Israelites mishandle God's Holy Objects and thousands die when the Ark returns. The ark is sent to Kirjathjearim for safe keeping, which was one of the Gibeonite towns saved from destruction when the Hittite population yielded to God. God took the Gibeonites on as servants under the supervision of the Levites after the Gibeonites confessed Him as their God.

1 Samuel 6:21 says, "And they sent messengers to the inhabitants of Kirjathjearim, saying, The Philistines have brought again the ark of the LORD; come ye down, and fetch it up to you." (KJV) In 1 Samuel 6.19 the book records that 50,090 Israelites die through the mishandling of the Ark when it is sent back by the Philistines. What could the Israelites have been thinking when they took a peak on the inside of the ark.

The Israelites are not about to sacrifice any more of their fellow kinsmen in the mishandling of the Ark, so they called for the Gibeonites to come fetch it. The Ark is sent to Abinadab's house and cared for by his son Eleazar. The people who lived in this town are the Hivites who are the Hittites who were the sons of Shem who were the sons of Canaan who were the sons of Ham. These Gibeonites were the servants of servants, the Nethinims. The Gibeonites in their service to the Levites learn how to care for the Holy Objects of God. It is quite possible that Uriah the Hittite lives in or near this community and is trained as a servant of servants in God's house. Little other explanation exists for

Uriah the Hittite's presence in this area of southern Palestine at this time in history.

The Gibeonite responsibility was to carry wood and water for the Levites. It is quite possible some of the wood and water is used for the service of the personal needs of the Levites, but wood and water's role in the service of God's House is a different matter. Within the Tabernacle, wood and water play a prominent role. The main courtyard of the Tabernacle contained the Bonze Laver and Alter of Burnt Offerings.

The Bronze Laver is a very large bronze wash basin polished to a mirror shine that contains water. The water was used to perform the ceremonial washing of the priests. The priest cannot be defiled with dirt or blood, so priests are continually required to wash in the performance their duties. The need for fresh water in the Bronze Laver is continuous due to the continual washing by the priest, so the "servant of servants", the Gibeonites, the Nethinims were keep busy replenishing the water supply. The old saying cleanliness is next to godliness probably gets its start with the Bronze Laver. While maintaining a clean exterior is important, the application of God to the interior is what is missing in the life of these Israelites.

In Mark 7:15 Jesus says, "There is nothing from without a man, that entering into him can defile him: but the things which come out of him, those are they that defile the man." (KJV) It is thought that the mirror finish to the inside the Bronze Laver produces a clear reflection so the Levites could see themselves as if looking in a mirror. There is nothing like a man looking himself straight in the face and examining himself that will produce a cleaner heart. 2 Corinthians 13:5 says, "Examine yourselves, whether ye be in the faith; prove your own selves. Know ye not your own selves, how that Jesus Christ is in you, except ye be reprobates?" (KJV)

Upon the Alter of the Burnt Offer the unblemished sacrifices are place to be consumed by the fire and to elevate the sweet savor of that sacrifice heavenly to God. The Alter of Burnt Offering requires a constant supply of wood to continue the Flame of the Lord, so the "servant of servants", the Gibeonites, the Nethinims are keep busy replenishing the wood supply. The wood consumption is tremendous due to the necessity of sustaining a temperature hot enough to completely consume all the flesh of every animal sacrifice. There is obviously a lot of Paul Bunyan in the Gibeonites after a few years of performing these duties. These Gibeonites are relatives of same giants with which Caleb dealt, so they were quite physically imposing fellows.

Uriah the Hittite is with little practical doubt a member of this servant of servant's caste and would have been taught a clear understanding of the significance the holy image presented in through the Bronze Laver and the Alter of Burnt Offerings. It is abundantly clear that the Gibeonites took their God and their role in God's service seriously. There is absolutely no reason God, after slaying 50,090 Israelites for mishandling His Holy Objects, to believe the same penalty would not be levied against the Gibeonites were they to fail in any of God's instructions regarding the care of His Holy objects. The Ark of God dwelt with the Gibeonites twenty years, before the hearts of Israel once again yearn for a touch from God.

Let us also recall that Uriah's name means "the flame of Jehovah." The flames at the Altar of Burnt Offerings consumed the sin offering. The servant of a servants' caste surely understood the symbolism represented in the Holy Objects of Worship. As a group during these early years in the Promised Land they are more devout in their study of the Holy Objects and worship of the Lord than most of the Hebrew children. A Gideonite's life depends on understanding God's rules for these objects. The Gibeonites could not have provided the Ark improper care and remained unharmed during their twenty year custody of the Ark were it otherwise.

So also as Christians we must take care to diligently follow God's instructions as we walk through the life with which he has entrusted us. God entrusts each Christian with the proper care of the physical temple, the human body, in which the Holy Spirit dwells. It is a serious responsibility that for every Christian to look into the Bronze Laver and examine him or herself. Sin is revealed during self-examination and must be expunged through the cleansing of the blood sacrifice supplied by our Lord Jesus Christ. No stench of a baby sin can be harbored in the Christian's heart. The burning offering is the sweet savior Christ's sacrifice carries to the very nostrils of God the Father, and the stench of our confessed sin is covered by Christ's fragrant smoke that fills heaven.

Chapter Seven

How does one grow up to be a mighty man?... it is the worst of times.

One should not forget what God remembers, and one should not remember what God forgets. For doing the first can surely kill you and doing the second can bring about judgment and death to your children. Uriah the Hittite is born into a society where this very drama plays out on a national stage. Uriah the Hittite survives the turmoil, death and destruction that surely touched many that are close to him, and these events have a direct impact on the plan God has for his life.

Uriah is to become one of King David's mighty men, and though David has been anointed by the prophet Samuel to become King, Uriah the Hittite comes into David's life after he has been anointed but prior to the actualization of David being placed on the throne. Events transpire that impacted Uriah the Hittite's life and bring him into David's service. The forgetting and remembering of Uriah's first king, King Saul, rips through the fabric of the nation and through Uriah's life.

The individual responsibility of sustaining a right relationship with a personal God is a level of accountability the nation is rejecting. The people are tired of judges telling them individually that they fail to remember God, and the people reject wholesale an intimate and personal relationship with God.

The people cry out for a fleshly King. These stiff-necked people no longer wanted to visit the judges like Samuel. The judges ruling over Israel settle disputes through the direct intervention of God in individual situations. The nation had co-mingled with sin for so long that the people wanted to escape the conviction of sin. The nation wanted to fill the spiritual vacuum of their godless hearts with a leader made of flesh. The nation of Israel wanted to practice nationhood in the energy of the flesh.

Major W. Ian Thomas in his classic The Mystery of Godliness says:

"The moment you come to realize that only God can make a man godly, you are left with no option, but to find God, and to know God, and to let God be God in you and through you, whoever He may be-and this will leave you no margin for picking and choosing- for there is only one God, and He is absolute, and He made you expressly for Himself!" (Thomas, 1964)

In a rewrite of this passage for Israel at this point in their nationhood and for the fallen world of today the passage might go something like:

The moment you choose to reject that only God that can make a man godly, you are left with no option, but to find a god like every other god, a god of your own choosing, and a god that lets you be god, and because you are god this leaves no margin for picking and choosing for that which you do is godly, and there is only one you, and you are absolute and you make yourself expressly for yourself.

When the nation gathers together by to hear from God through Samuel about their fleshly king, 1 Samuel 10:17-19 says:

"And Samuel called the people together unto the LORD to Mizpeh; And said unto the children of Israel, Thus saith the LORD God of Israel, I brought up Israel out of Egypt, and delivered you out of the hand of the Egyptians, and out of the hand of all kingdoms, [and] of them that oppressed you: And ye have this day rejected your God, who himself saved you out of all your adversities and your tribulations; and ye have said unto him, Nay, but set a king over us. Now therefore present yourselves before the LORD by your tribes, and by your thousands." (KJV)

So the nation in the days of Uriah the Hittite is apostate and far from having a relationship with God. The nation chooses to abandon their faith in God and His leadership. God even shares with the nation that the king they so desire will suck the life out of the nation, and when the nation finally cries out for God to intervene on their behalf, "the Lord will not hear you in that day" I Samuel 8.18. Even after God protests through a direct appeal from Samuel to the nation, the nation spits in God's eye.

So God allows the nation a king that is made to order for a flesh driven nation. The English Standard Bible's translation describes Saul, the newly to be crowned king, well. I Samuel 9.2 says, "And he (Kish) had a son whose name is Saul, a handsome young man. There is not a man among the people of Israel more handsome than he. From his shoulders upward he is taller than any of the people." (ESB)

Saul is the hottest hotty in the entire nation. Saul stood out in the crowd because the next tallest person in the entire country only came to his shoulder. Saul is the best piece of eye candy in the entire country. The men envied Saul's good looks and the women palpitated over Saul as they flipped through his swim suit edition.

Saul is on the surface a fine physical specimen. The human rule of thumb seems to always yield to the idea that bigger is better. Saul's physical prowess would make him a good match for all those nasty Philistine giants that live over by Gath. In the eyes of a flesh driven nation Saul is the best piece of flesh that could be found, and he is to be their champion against their enemies.

But what do we find on Saul's resume or his pedigree that would suggest that he would make a fit leader of the nation? Let us first review the heritage from which this new king spawns.

Saul's pedigree is, as already mention, of the tribe of Benjamin. Most casual Bible readers will remember Benjamin as Joseph's younger brother and that Benjamin is not involved in the dirty deed perpetrated on Joseph that sent Joseph as a slave to Egypt. But this last and most spoiled child of Jacob spawned a tribe of rotten offspring that even the apostate eleven other tribes could not stomach.

In the Old Testament Book of Judges a story of the Tribe of Benjamin unfolds in chapters 19 and 20. The story starts with a not so godly Levite who takes up with a not so godly concubine. The Levite has taken the concubine home to be his wife only to have her play the whore. After sleeping around the Levite's concubine runs home to daddy for protection because her dallying requires a death sentence. Finally after four months the Levite decides to go to his father-in-law's home and take back his wife.

The concubine's father entertains the Levite for six days. The excessive hospitality is an effort to earn forgiveness for his daughter's deplorable behavior. We might also assume that the concubine's father is well aware of the Levitical law allowing the Levite to put his daughter to death for her adultery. Even the father of a rotten daughter will have his heart wrench when considering the thought that her imminent departure may well be the last time his eyes will fall upon that sweet child he once hugged and kissed.

After six days the Levite and concubine depart getting a very late start on the day. Travel is fraught with danger in those days especially after dark, so the Levite chose a Hebrew town to spend the night thinking he would find safety therein. The town is Gibeah and is of the Tribe of Benjamin. Gibeah is King Saul's hometown.

Godly hospitality is demanded for the traveler in those times, but no man in Gibeah extended hospitality to this man of the cloth and his wife for the night. Not one Benjaminite offered up a cold glass of water to this weary couple. So as the sun is setting the Levite and his wife are sitting like bums in the street considering on which park bench to sleep.

As the sun slips over the horizon an old man returns to his home from working outside of the town. Knowing the wicked character of his Benjaminite neighbors the old man hopes to avoid trouble for the travelers by offering them the opportunity to spend the night in his home. As the old man and Levite dine his Gibeah neighbors gin up their debauchery to the point it pours out to the street.

Judges 19:22 states, "Now as they the old man and Levite were making their hearts merry, behold, the men of the city, certain sons of Belial, beset the house round about, and beat at the door, and space to the master of the house, the old man, saying, Bring forth the man that came into thine house, that we may know him." (KJV)

First let us note that these men of Gibeah, these Benjaminites, are called the sons of Belial. Belial is not a place and it is not a person. Character does matter and Belial speaks to the nature and character of these men of Gibeah, these forefathers of Saul.

Belial means godless men. So these residents of Gibeah are not only godless men, but they were sons of godless men. Two generations or more of godless living is boiling up inside these Benjaminites.

The Benjaminites are soon pounding on the doors and windows of the old man's house demanding that the Levite be sent outside so "that we may know him." A gang of godless men demand that the Levite exit the house and be sodomized. The depth of the vileness in demanding the Levite present himself is nearly beyond comprehension, and yet these Benjaminites are from whom Saul counts his ancestry.

But the story does not end with the threat of sodomizing male rape. The old man offers up his daughter and the Levite's concubine in an appeasing effort to avoid the gang raping and sodomizing the Levite. The Benjaminites in their perversion driven anger forgo the old man's daughter and take only the Levite's concubine.

The concubine spends the night being repeated brutalized by this gang of godless Benjaminites. By how many men she is taken is not known. But the trauma of repeated rapes causes significant internal physical damage to the women. The concubine is discarded in front of the old man's house and crawls to the door. Too weak to raise a hand and knock on the door she dies with her face in the dust and hands extended as if begging for help on the door's threshold.

In the morning the Levite in a sham speaks to his dead wife and then throws her on the donkey. The Levite is in a hurry to return to work so he feigns she is not dead. Touching the dead body would make the Levite ceremonially unclean and unfit for his religious duties. It is the very reason the rabbi pasted by the robbed and bludgeoned man lying in the ditch in the New Testament story of the Good Samaritan.

The story still does not end. The wickedness of Gibeah and its Benjaminites spread. For when the Levite does return to his community he decides not to go to work but instead returns to his home with his dead wife. After the long ride the Levite decides punishment is due the sodomites of Gibeah. The Levite cuts the body of his wife into twelve pieces. The Levite then sends one of the twelve pieces to each of the twelve tribes of Israel. The Levite demands Gibeah and its sodomites be punishment for acts beyond the pale for even the most jaded of the Israelites.

The tribe of Benjamin receives its piece of the concubine's body. The heinous acts of debauchery and murder are shared with the Benjaminites as with the other eleven tribes. When the men of Israel gathered outside Gibeah, in one voice they demand the Benjaminites give up the gang raping murders for punishment. But the sons of godless men are not about to give up their godless sons. These Benjaminites, these sons of Belial, gather and refuse any guilt on the part of the gang bangers. The Tribe of Benjamin chooses to protect those who perpetrated this heinous action rather than give them up for punishment. To protect their own deviants the Tribe of Benjamin wages war against their fellow Israelites.

During the first two days the Benjaminites experienced a degree of success prosecuting the battle to protect this godless lot of buggers. It seems the Israelites start wondering what is up given the battle is not faring well. So in Judges 20.28 the high priest

Phinehas, the grandson of Moses' brother Aaron, finally decides to ask God what is up. Phinehas's answer comes directly, "And the LORD said, Go up; for tomorrow I will deliver them into thine hand." (KJV) Well when God delivered the Benjaminites, He delivered every last one of the godless sons of godless sons. As is the case when God delivered previous of His enemies for destruction, He wanted them completely eradicated. No sin was to remain.

Israel stopped before the job is finished. The Israelites allowed that which God delivered for execution to escape punishment. The Benjaminites that survive are six hundred of the fastest running cowards in all of Israel. These six hundred Benjaminite men do not fight to save the lives of their fathers, mothers, wives and children. These weasels ran into the wilderness to the rock of Rimmon and hid their sorry butts. Like rodents seeking protection from birds of prey these beasts masquerading as men hid amongst the rocks. These cowards hid for four months. Hunger and thirst were probably the only forces able to bring this spineless lot to the light of day.

So a Benjaminite cancer for which God provided a cure is left incompletely circumcised. Once hearing the physician's dreadful diagnosis of a large cancerous tumor needing immediate surgical removal, when does it make any sense for a patient to say, 'Doctor those cancer cells have been a part of me for quite some time, and I believe they are meant to be part of me. Doc, I don't want you to cut the entire tumor out of me. Leave a little of it in me. I don't believe the cancer you'll leave in me will cause me any future problems."

The insanity of Israel to not completely cutting out and utterly destroying this Benjaminite cancer explodes into the almost incomprehensible national discussion on how to help the cancer recover. The Israelites concoct a plan to propagate the Tribe of Benjamin, the tribe God delivered to them for destruction.

There is an old anonymously written Negro spiritual entitled *Don't Let The Devil Ride*, and these are the lyrics:

Don't Let The Devil Ride

Don't let the Devil ride
Oh don't let the devil ride
'Cause if you <u>let him</u> ride
He'll want to try to drive
Don't let him ride

Don't let him flag you down
If he flags you down
He'll <u>turn</u> your soul around
Don't let him ride

Don't let him be your boss
If you let him be your boss
He'll make your soul be lost
Don't let him ride

Don't let him ride with you
If he ride with you
He'll tell what to do
Don't let him ride

Israel lets the devil ride that day when God's orders are not followed to the letter. The Israelites became comfortable with the idea of co-existing with this cancer that is killing them. This satanic passenger actually gets Israel to turn around. The surviving 600 godless Benjaminites are provided godless wives from outside Israel, so as a cancer Benjamin can once again flourish.

Saul, descends from godless sons of godless sons, descends from a cancer God ordered Israel to destroy, and descends from one of six hundred cowards who intermarried with godless women. Saul is to be the people's choice for King. If you let him be your boss he'll make your soul be lost. If he ride with you he'll tell you what to do, don't let the devil ride. But ride, oh no he does. Now the devil is to be the boss. The devil is no longer to ride, the devil is to drive. Though our heritage plays a significant role in our lives, we must not forget it is our responsibility to choose.

How often does the world seem to control much of our lives? Uriah is a young man growing up in a peaceful town working at the tabernacle when Saul is made king. Serving the temple had been the work of Uriah's people for hundreds of years. Not unlike many of rural American farm boys whose worlds are forever changed by Hitler and World War II, Uriah's shady days at the fishing hole with his buckets of water are about to be exchanged for the bloody hedge row fighting at Normandy. The normalcy of going with friends to a dance is forever loss in the empty stares of lifeless face on the battlefield. Uriah's world is about to come crashing down around him as the devil through the hands of King Saul is about to take the reins of Israel and drive the country still further into a spiritual ditch.

Chapter Eight

How does one grow up to be a mighty man? The devil is about to drive Uriah's country.

Saul comes from a family of wealth and influence. So when you drive by Saul's family's home it has curb appeal. Saul's family was one of the biggest fish in the nation's smallest pond. So Saul had it all in the eyes of the world. He had looks, he had money, and he had the power and influence of a wealthy well placed family. Saul was a good political choice because his tribe hadn't the power to exert undue influence over any of the other tribes. Saul was the proverbial trust fund baby.

But what was on the inside of Saul once the smoke cleared and the band stop playing Pomp and Circumstance?

There is no mention of Saul's virtue. No mention of Saul's exemplary character traits are shared in the Bible. Nothing is told of how well he scores in his Jewish catechism classes. Saul was a grown man with a family, yet he remained in his father Kish's house. The only job experience that Saul brought to the table that was worthy of mention in the Bible was that he was a failed herder of asses.

To many a fan of old western movies, Kish sent his son Saul on a round-up. Saul was also apparently a quite proud fellow and may not have recognized the difficulty of droving asses over, around and through mountainous areas. His father recognizing his son to be ass herder challenged, so the father found it necessary to tell Saul to take some help along with him. It is important to note that Saul didn't recognize his ass herder shortcomings and had to be directed to take help. Romans 12:3 says, "For I say, through the grace given unto me, to every man that is among you, not to think of himself more highly than he ought to think; but to think soberly, according as God hath dealt to every man the measure of faith." (KJV)

Round-up can be a long, dirty and physically demanding job. It requires a great deal of time and effort. Animals left to wander can stray for miles foraging subsistence. As the story goes Saul packs provisions and starts wandering all over the country looking for his father's lost asses. Saul also never asked for help from anyone during this search and that included the servant sent along to help.

Saul could not find the wandering asses he was suppose to round-up and herd back to the homestead, so we don't even know whether Saul could herd asses. What we do discover is Saul is proud and is a quitter. Saul is willing to return home after just three days searching without these valuable family assets thus leaving the task his father had assigned him undone. He was willing to quit his task and head for home without asking for help.

When Saul was fed-up trying to find the asses and nearly out of provisions, he started to head for home. Saul's story is that he is concerned that his father would be worried that some ill-fate may have befallen him. Kish apparently had successfully owned foraging herd animals for a lifetime. Kish understood the time and labor intensive nature of the task he had assigned Saul, yet it does appear that after several days Kish was becoming concerned about his son's safety. Yet a task is over when it is over and not before. This character flaw of Saul's did not change through his life. This character flaw was never to be redeemed throughout Saul's life. Saul consistently quit on God, and went whining back to his old ways.

Again Saul's first inclination was to head for home, to retreat back to his earthly father's house. It was Saul's servant that suggests insight ought to be sought from God through the prophet Samuel about the location of the lost asses. When his servant made the suggestion to visit Samuel, Saul's first concern regarding an interaction with Samuel was how to pay for the services. Saul's first interaction with God is marked by the perspective that the God of Israel's services are up for sale.

1Samuel 9:7-8 and 10 say, "Then said Saul to his servant, But, behold, if we go, what shall we bring the man? For the bread is spent in our vessels, and there is not a present to bring to the man of God: what have we? And the servant answered Saul again, and said, Behold, I have here at hand the fourth part of a shekel of silver: [that] will I give to the man of God, to tell us our way. Then said Saul to his servant, Well said; come, let us go. So they went unto the city where the man of God was." (KJV)

So Saul and the servant hatch what they think is a good plan. The pair would seek out the prophet Samuel and pay the seer a shekel of silver for his services. Saul knows so little of God that he thinks God will serve money.

In Act 8:20-23 a story is recorded regarding the condition of a man's heart who wanted to purchase the services of God: "But Peter said unto him, Thy money perish with thee, because thou hast thought that the gift of God may be purchased with money. Thou hast neither part nor lot in this matter: for thy heart is not right in the sight of God. Repent therefore of this thy wickedness, and pray God, if perhaps the thought of thine heart may be forgiven thee. For I perceive that thou art in the gall of bitterness, and [in] the bond of iniquity." (KJV)

So the nation of Israel is about to receive a king of their own choosing. Saul looks great on the outside, but a heart of this world beat in his chest. Saul is the embodiment of the foul and fallen desire of their hearts.

When God chooses a king or a saint, He doesn't look from the outside inward but from the inside outward. 1Samuel 16:7 says "But the LORD said unto Samuel, Look not on his countenance, or on the height of his stature; because I have refused him: for the LORD seeth not as man seeth; for man looketh on the outward appearance, but the LORD looketh on the heart." (KJV)

Isn't it funny how a flesh driven man always believes he is in the driver's seat. How a man believes he chooses the course, the path, his life is taking. Nary has a child who studies literature in an American public school not read the country's poet laureate Robert Frost's classic:

The Road Not Taken

Two roads diverged in a yellow wood,
And sorry I could not travel both
And be one traveler, long I stood
And looked down one as far as I could
To where it bent in the undergrowth;

Then took the other, as just as fair,
And having perhaps the better claim
Because it was grassy and wanted wear;

Though as for that the passing there
Had worn them really about the same,

And both that morning equally lay
In leaves no step had trodden black.
Oh, I kept the first for another day!
Yet knowing how way leads on to way,
I doubted if I should ever come back.

I shall be telling this with a sigh
Somewhere ages and ages hence:
Two roads diverged in a wood, and I—
I took the one less traveled by,
And that has made all the difference.

This is the heart of a fallen man, "and I- I took the one less traveled by." I made the decision. My decisions as a traveler through life make all the difference. There is not one prayer offered up for divine guidance. Not one thought of a God who sees even the sparrow fall to the ground in the undergrowth. This man is just a lone traveler, solitary and isolated, deciding to take the less traveled road.

"How way leads on to way" or how one chance roll of the dice randomly leads to another the traveler thinks to himself. I will save the second road for another day, as he blindly plods down the road without one thought given to his Maker's interest in his life. Chance will probably not bring me this way again the traveler thinks, but if I ever pass this way again I'll save the first road for that day.

I Samuel 9.15-16 says, "Now the LORD had told Samuel in his ear a day before Saul came, saying, Tomorrow about this time I will send thee a man out of the land of Benjamin..." (KJV)

So Saul is about to be stuck with a fork, but it is not Robert Frost's fork in the road. It is the divine fork of Godly intervention into the life of Saul. So, is all of life just random chance, a series of forks in the road as Robert Frost would have us believe?

Did the wandering Saul's servant grasp a wayward thought when suggesting a visit to the prophet? Did these two peer just far enough down Frost's fork in the road? Was it to be a trip back to Kish or a trip to Samuel? Were the asses for which they sought ever lost if God sees every sparrow in the entire world's undergrowth? Is this a free will or God's divine direction? God said, "I will send....."

Samuel knows Saul before Saul had the first thought of Samuel. Samuel knows Saul is coming for a visit before Saul decides to go looking for Samuel. Samuel has a feast prepared for Saul when Saul thought his supply amounted to a crust of bread and a coin in his pocket.

So Saul and his servant find the prophet Samuel and before the two could ask their first asinine question Samuel tells the pair they are coming to dinner. Samuel follows the dinner invitation with a couple of statements. The prophet first states that tomorrow he is going to tell Saul about his future. Secondly, and almost offhandedly, Samuel says, "Oh by the way, those lost asses you been looking for, they are found and are being held for you."

Now, can't you hear Saul thinking to himself, "How did Samuel know I was looking for my father's lost asses? What is going on? I didn't come here to have my fortune told?" But before Saul has a chance to blurt out something stupid Samuel speaks again.

Samuel asks Saul if he understands that the hope on a nation is now on him and his father's house. Here the prophet of God tells Saul out of the blue that the nation is counting on him. Saul's utters a response straight out of the flesh. Saul states my family is pretty small to be taking on the responsibility of a national leadership role. I'm not sure my family and I are capable of playing at that level. Again Saul's character flaw of looking back to his earthly father's house for sustenance is evident. Rather than looking forward to support from the God for which Samuel speaks Saul relies on his own resources.

So Samuel and Saul dine with thirty other dinner guests. Samuel continued his conversation with Saul into the cool of the evening on a Middle Eastern version of a veranda. The Bible does not share how soundly Saul slept that evening, but his alarm clock the following morning was Samuel telling Saul to get on his way, he's burning daylight.

As Saul departs Samuel walks with him bidding Saul's servant to travel on ahead. Samuel anoints Saul to be captain over God's inheritance. Samuel also confirms the anointing with prophesy through an advanced description of the events of the coming day, so Saul has confirmation on top of confirmation. Saul is also given very specific instructions about a future event that will be easily recognized when the events occur. Saul is given specific instructions on exactly how he is to perform his duties in that time and place. Saul may not have been sure he wasn't on a high from a spiked drink consumed at the previous night's dinner.

As Christians when God speaks to our hearts we must listen and respond. Many Christians too often are so wrapped up in themselves and their day to day business that God's speaking to their lives is brushed away with little more thought and attention given an irritating nat. When the Holy Spirit speaks to you in any one of the millions of voices with which He communicates with men and women, pay attention and act in faith on the charge given by God's speaking. People's lives are impacted by that which we both do and don't do when God calls us to action.

God puts men and women in tough circumstances. Saul's coming spiritual failures will destroy Uriah the Hittite's family and community. Uriah will serve God throughout his coming trials whereas Saul will not serve God in his blessing.

Chapter Nine

How does one grow up to be a mighty man? The worst of times are about to get worse.

Saul is not God's choice for the job. In spite of every effort God makes to help Saul see a bright new future he cannot take his eyes off the past.

Saul and his servant depart from the prophet Samuel. The prophecy Samuel delivers to Saul has a travel itinerary for that fateful day. Specific locations are to be visited. The first location is the sepulcher of Rachel, the second location is the oak of Tabor (the weeping oak of Deborah), and the third is Gibeath-elohim. Saul's prophetic journey that day takes him to a grave, a tree and a hill of God. It seems a bit of a strange journey.

Saul is a Benjaminite. Saul's family descended from the tribe of Benjamin. Benjamin is the last of Jacob's twelve sons. Rachel is Jacob's favorite wife and the mother of both his last two children Joseph and Benjamin.

A visit to Genesis chapter 29 recounts Rachel's story. Jacob is sent by his mother to her brother Laban's house as a result of Jacob's deceptive theft of Esau's birthright. Jacob finds his way to Laban's house and quickly falls in love with Laban's youngest daughter Rachel. Rachel is a beautiful women and Saul probably came by his good looks through Rachel.

Jacob strikes an agreement with Laban for Rachel's hand in marriage. For the privilege of marrying Rachel Jacob agrees to work for Laban seven years. Upon completion of those seven years there is a marriage. The seeds of deception Jacob had planted in stealing his brother's birthright come home to roost. Laban substitutes Rachel's older ugly sister Leah as Jacob's bride. Leah's face is hidden behind a veil through which Jacob cannot see. The deception is not unlike the ruse Jacob perpetrated on his own father Isaac. Isaac's eyesight had greatly failed and Jacob had disguised himself as his brother Esau to receive this father's blessing given to the first born son.

Jacob is forced to labor seven more years in Laban's charge to receive Rachel's hand in marriage. Soon after Jacob tires of Laban's involvement in his house and he decides to secretly leave Laban's dominance one night. When Rachel is made aware of the departure she looks back to her father's house, and she steals her father's idols during the stealthy nocturnal departure. Laban awakes to find Jacob, his daughters and his idols missing. Laban gives chase and runs down Jacob's fleeing family.

Jacob is unaware of Rachel's theft of Laban's idols. When Laban accuses Jacob of the theft, Jacob allows Laban the freedom to search his belongings and then pronounces a curse. The New Living Translation translates Genesis 31.32 Jacob's curse as, "But as for your gods, see if you can find them, and let the person who has taken them die!" (NLV) Jacob places the curse of death on the thief. Even Shakespeare did not write a more tragic turn of events for Jacob condemns unaware the love of his life, the beautiful Rachel, to death for the theft of Laban's idols. Though Rachel is able to delay her death sentence through her own deceit judgment soon overtakes the lying lips of the fairest of fair Rachel.

So why of all the locations God could direct Saul on this journey did He first take him to the grave of a dead great-something grandmother. As explored earlier one should not forget what God remembers, and one should not remember what God forgets. To do the first can surely kill you, and to do the second can bring judgment on and death to your children.

The God of Creation is literally yelling from the tree tops. Saul take a look around. Look what happened to Rachel. Rachel did not leave her old life behind. Rachel held on to her old life, her old gods, and it killed her. Rachel looks back instead of looking forward. Rachel would not forget what God said to forget. Rachel turns back and attempts to bring her old life into her new life. You cannot put new wine in old wine skins because the new wine bursts the old wine skins.

Learn from this place God is shouting to Saul. I am the way, the truth and the light. Remember that people die when they don't remember who to have faith in. There is a memorial built here at this gravesite. This place not only marks where an ancestor of yours is buried, this place shouts a remembrance of the impact of the failure to keep your eyes on the God of your future.

Don't look back Saul. Don't let the devil ride Saul. If you let the devil ride Saul he is going to want to drive Saul. Look what happened to Rachel Saul! Saul, you have the same problem that has been passed down to you from Rachel. Don't look back like Rachel, don't you look to your earthly father for strength in this journey. Stop Saul, stop looking back to your old way of thinking and look forwarded to a new life with Me as your guide. Remember what I remember, God attempts through this Rachel example to pound into Saul's head. God knows He has a big test coming up for Saul. Saul will have to remember this day at Rachel's grave; remember that failure to remember when test day arrives means failure on the exam.

The second visit Saul is to make on this day of prophetic revelation is a visit to the Oak of Tabor. One hundred and fifty years ago there was published in the long defunct magazine The British Mothers' Journal and Domestic Magazine, Volumes 5-6 a short piece authored by a J. Bakewell.

The article entitled The Pious Nurse is repeated hear:

"The Bible, which has erected so many monuments to record the worth of distinguished virtue, has not passed by the pious nurse. The sacred narrative says, "But Deborah, Rebakak's nurse, died: and she is buried beneath Bethel, under an oak; and the name of it is called *Allon-bachuth*" (the oak of Weeping). There is something very beautiful in this short piece of biography, and far more valuable than many volumes of wars, the political intrigues, and follies which are generally the staple of history. We should notice that it is "Rebakak's nurse." She had nursed Jacob's mother, and had now lived in the family upward of sixty years. She had left Mesopotamia many years before, to accompany her young mistress. She had nursed and waited on Rebekah, and probably had closed her eyes in death, and, having laid her in the grave, had returned to her native land again, and had taken up her abode in the family of her young master Jacob; and now behold, although her head is gray, she had a second time quitted her native land for ever, that she might end her days in the family to which she is so much attached. It may be that that she hoped for a grave near that of her mistress, but God's providence obtained otherwise, and she died on the road; while her worth gave immortality to *Allon-bachuth*, "the oak of weeping," the new appellation of the oak gave immortality to her virtues. I can conceive of no epitaph equal to this. Its brevity, pathos, and comprehensiveness cannot not be surpassed. It tells us that there is great weeping in the house of Jacob. Deborah had the affection of all. Jacob wept for her as for a mother; his surviving wives and children wept; and even the other domestics wept when the aged Deborah died, and is carried to her grave. "The oak of weeping," therefore, became an appropriate monument for the venerable Deborah. Her name signifies "a female oracle," and it is not unlikely that she is the chronicle and prophetess of the family. When our love of novels and fiction shall give place to the more beautiful and interesting realities of truth, and we shall become an intellectual and moral age, so that the lovely and touching narratives of female virtue, as exhibited in the affection and piety of tender-hearted daughters, mothers, wives, and female attendants, shall be more captivating than the sentimental woe of the love-sick dame; then the pious historian and biographer will be able to enchant his readers with the memorials of many a Deborah."

A life of pious service is honored at this "the oak of weeping. Saul is told that his leadership is to be subject to God. God will provide Saul guidance through Samuel. Saul is in the service of God. Saul's life is to be a life of serving the nation that is God's inheritance. The oak shouted out humility, service and piety above self interest. Would the tears that soaked the ground at this grave of Deborah call out to the heart of the newly anointed King? Would Saul sense the magnitude of God sending him to this precious place on this day of his anointing? Would Saul learn a lesson from the gift of charity extended to him by those he meets at the weeping oak or will he move into his kingship gradually think more highly of himself than he ought?

The last of Saul's stops on this fateful and prophetic day is "the hill of God". This hill is apparently very close to Saul's home town of Gibeah, and perhaps he could view it from his father

Kish's property. The "hill of God" housed a seminary that taught prophecy. Also on the same hill is a garrison of Philistine soldiers who cohabitated on the same hilltop with a God they hated but feared. Perhaps it is the memory of their deity Dagon lying face down in the dust next to the Ark of the Covenant that tempered their hostility and extended their respect. Perhaps it is the memory of the plague of emerods, the pustule sores that afflicted their penises and anuses when the Ark of the Covenant remained in their hands. However begrudging the respect, the respect is paid by the Philistine soldiers in honor of the Lord God of Israel through the peaceful sharing of a strategic hilltop.

Recall Gibeah from its previous mention as the Benjaminite story in Judge's chapter 20 is related in chapter 7. Yes this is the town that viciously raped and murdered the Levite's wayward wife because the Levite would not present himself to the men of the town to be sodomized. This is the town that the tribe of Benjamin protected in spite of their evil deeds. This is the town that on the third day of battle is ordered slaughtered by God. Not one Benjaminite is to have survived that day. The only survivors of that day were cowards that hide amongst the rocks like rodents. The Benjaminites then married Canaanite women to restore their population.

Now here is Saul walking over "the hill of God" while Philistines posted a garrison of soldiers on the same patch of ground. The same call goes out to the heart of Saul at this location as had occurred at the other stops. Look back to the ways your Canaanite mothers and the gods they brought with them to Gibeah or look forward to leadership of and worship to the God of Israel.

Remember, the eleven other tribes of Israel had sworn not to give their daughters to the sons of Benjamin for wives. For several generations these sons of Beliel married into the Canaanite population. As was Rachael's desire when she stole her father Laban's idols, these women brought with them the gods with whom they had been raised. These wives as mothers had raised their children to worship these idols. Would these godless sons of Benjamin actually worship the God of Israel Who had ordered their extinction? Would Saul yield to the prophetic call God is about to shower on him, or would a Benjaminite cancer rage through the nation.

Saul is about to be provided a cure for the cancer that has been left completely untreated in his life. Three times Saul hears the physician's dreaded diagnosis of a large cancerous tumor needing immediate surgical removal. Will Saul say this prophetic day cut it all out Lord or will this patient say, 'Doctor those cancer cells have been a part of me for quite some time, and I believe they are meant to be part of me. Doc, I don't want you to cut the entire tumor out of me. Leave a little of it in me. I don't believe the cancer you'll leave in me will cause me any future problems."

God wants all of your past left behind. Christians are born again. Christians yield all to Jesus Christ. The road to healing is leaving behind that which caused the illness and fully accepting Jesus whose embrace gives life to those that yield. Christians should not attempt to hold onto that which God desires to cut out of their lives. The short term pain of the knife yields everlasting joy. Let that harbored sin go, and embrace God's healing.

Uriah the Hittite yields to God's call. Uriah could have become consumed by the bitterness and hate of all the unfair events that chronicled his life, but he did not. Uriah let go of the poison. Uriah served his God to the end.

Chapter Ten

How does one grow up to be a mighty man? When your earthly leadership and country is full of cancer your eyes can only be for the one true God.

Saul's travel itinerary includes the meeting with several people. In each meeting there is an exchange between those God has positioned to interact with Saul. I Samuel 10:1-6 relates the activities that God has planned for Saul and prophesied through Samuel.

"Then Samuel took a vial of oil, and poured it upon his head, and kissed him, and said, Is it not because the LORD hath anointed thee to be captain over his inheritance? When thou art departed from me to day, then thou shalt find two men by Rachel's sepulchre in the border of Benjamin at Zelzah; and they will say unto thee, The asses which thou wentest to seek are found: and, lo, thy father hath left the care of the asses, and sorroweth for you, saying, What shall I do for my son? Then shalt thou go on forward from thence, and thou shalt come to the plain of Tabor, and there shall meet thee three men going up to God to Bethel, one carrying three kids, and another carrying three loaves of bread, and another carrying a bottle of wine: And they will salute thee, and give thee two loaves of bread; which thou shalt receive of their hands. After that thou shalt come to the hill of God, where is the garrison of the Philistines: and it shall come to pass, when thou art come thither to the city, that thou shalt meet a company of prophets coming down from the high place with a psaltery, and a tabret, and a pipe, and a harp, before them; and they shall prophesy: And the Spirit of the LORD will come upon thee, and thou shalt prophesy with them, and shalt be turned into another man."(KJV)

Saul is anointed for his new role by Samuel and turns to depart. I Samuel 10:9 states that when Saul turns to leave God gives him another heart. Strong's Concordance indicates that God overthrows or overturns what was in Saul's heart. God apparently frees Saul from all the roots of bitterness that cloud his understanding of the world and of God's operation in the world. Saul's inner man, his mind, his will, his understanding is free to absorb that which God is doing in and about his world.

In Chapter Nine the location of Saul's first stop at Rachel's sepulcher is discussed. Saul meets two men who have a personal message for him. This entire course of events starts with Saul departing his father's house to look for several lost asses. Saul and his servant nearly gave up the quest to find the lost asses when their provisions had run out and when Saul fears that his father may have become worried about his well being.

The prophecy Saul receives from Samuel and the message two men are to deliver at Rachel's sepulcher is, "The asses which thou wentest to seek are found: and, lo, thy father hath left the care of the asses, and sorroweth for you, saying, What shall I do for my son?"

So the two men verify for to Saul that the asses for which he had been sent to search are now returned to his father. So any latent concern that may have been rumbling around in the back of Saul's head about the asses is relieved. God has sent Saul a prophecy and a confirmation of that prophecy. The property for which he sought is now safe. Saul has been given a mind that can understand God's intervention. God is taking care of Saul and the country he is to lead. God is concerned and cares for even the farm animals. God provided Saul with a banquet and shelter at Samuel's house when he is down to his last dollar and far from home. God provides Saul and the nation their physical needs. God calls out to Saul, as He does to us today, from Philippians in the New King James translation, "Be anxious for nothing, but in everything by prayer and supplication, with thanksgiving, let your requests be made known to God." (NKJV) In the New Living Translation the verse is a little more transparent, "Don't worry about anything; instead, pray about everything. Tell God what you need, and thank him for all he has done." (NLV)

The second concern discussed in this exchange at Rachel's sepulcher is a look back at Saul's father. Saul apparently knew his earthly father fairly well, and Saul's concern from a little over a day ago is revisited when speaking with these two men. The question for Saul at Rachel's sepulcher is will I put my trust in the God. Can Saul recognize God's intervention in his life? Saul must trust God to be king and to lead Israel. Or, is this newly met God not big enough to calm the heart of his earthly father as Saul goes about God's business? Will Saul hold onto the anxiety and fear of his earthly father or will he trust in his heavenly Father with his earthly father's mental health and peace? Will he remain encumbered and weighed down by a past without God, or will Saul reject those old idols and embrace a future where God knows the location of lost farm animals and can guide the farm animals home without anxiety?

Does it at anytime seem to click with Saul that the events of the past few days are orchestrated by the God who memorialized Himself to His chosen people through His name, I AM? Did it ever occur to Saul that the God of gods Who could elevate a timid and confused farmer to the throne of a nation could surely enable the same man to rule that nation? So why not start now Saul? Why not start with trusting the worries of an earthly parent to your heavenly Father? Start by releasing the Benjaminite propensity to not trust God, yes that propensity burned into the Benjaminite heart. Leave behind the long harbored and nurtured bitterness towards God for the death of Rachael that has consumed your tribe for generations. Trust the God that sanctioned the elimination of all your Benjaminite ancestors because of the sin practiced in your hometown. Release the bitterness towards God that is now a deadly cancer in the Benjaminite heart. Start by believing God will care for your earthly dad. Trust God with more than the safe return of the asses. Put your trust in God for the well being of your father, your nation and your life.

Saul travels to Rachel's sepulcher and sure enough there are a couple of fellows that meet up with him there. Does it not seem a bit strange that God would direct Saul to the tomb of a woman who died specifically because she looked back and would not leave her past in the past? She would not forget what God wanted her to forget, she would not embrace the future that her husband's God had planned for her. She had placed her trust in the impotent gods of her father, and it produced her death.

In contrast the weeping place of the pious Deborah is juxtaposed. A life of selfless service was honored. A woman whose love for others overpowered any desire to advance herself. A woman who lets go of all that was behind to follow and serve Abraham and his family. Deborah was the women who did not look back. Saul, God calls out from this place of weeping, don't look back. Follow Deborah's example, follow Me.

1Samuel 10:6, "And the Spirit of the LORD will come upon thee, and thou shalt prophesy with them, and shalt be turned into another man." (KJV)

And Saul did prophesy with the prophets coming down the "hill of God" into his hometown. It was such a strange sight to his friends and neighbors that that the New Living Bible describes their shock best in 1 Samuel 10:12, "And one of those standing there said, Can anyone become a prophet, no matter who his father is?" (KJV)

The Spirit of God came quickly upon Saul, but the Spirit was not to stay on Saul. While the Spirit rested upon Saul, he prophesied with the boldness of the accompanying prophet. But it was to be a short event. When Saul heard his friends and family start talking about his new found religion, Saul stops prophesying and Saul retreats to a "high place." A "high place" often denotes a place of worship.

Was this "high place" to which Saul retreats the same high place from which he had just descended? It seems to be a place of worship that Saul's uncle feels comfortable enough about to following Saul there. The Benjaminite crowd took serious note of the religious crowd with whom Saul was traveling because it was something they had not before seen Saul do, yet locals did not take particular note of Saul's steps to the "high place" once he returned home.

Why so little interest in his worship at the local "high place"? Why the concern about Saul's throwing in with the Samuel crowd? Why no discussion of the unusual nature of Saul's actions when he retreats to this local "high place?

Why?

Saul retreats to a "high place" to which he is familiar. Saul retreats to a "high place" to which his uncle is familiar. Saul retreats to a 'high place" with which the crowd is familiar. He returns to the place of his former worship, his uncle's worship and his brethren's worship. He returns to the spot of idol worship his brethren find unalarming. Saul looks back to the ways of Rachel, he returns to the idols of his mother and father. When confronted with making a testimony for the God of Abraham, Isaac and Jacob, he hides in the comfort of the old idols. The enemy of Saul's soul attacks him with fear and he turns away from publicly testifying of what God is doing in his life.

What drives men and women to return to the failings of their sin? "Matthew Henry wonders, "How apt are sinners to taste God and turn away. Pro 26:11 says, "As a dog returneth to his vomit, [so] a fool returneth to his folly." As the dog, after he has gained ease by vomiting that which burdened his stomach, yet goes and licks it up again, so sinners, who have been convinced only and not converted, return to sin again, forgetting how sick it made them. The apostle in 2 Pt. 2:22 applies this proverb to those that have known the way of righteousness but are turned from it; but God will spew them out of his mouth, Rev. 3:16." (Henry)

In Saul's first big test his fear and lack of trust in Jehovah causes him to lose a hereditary kingdom that would have lasted forever. Saul is given specific instruction to wait for Samuel prior to taking any action against a Philistine attack. Saul fails to wait on Samuel. With each passing day Saul's numbers became fewer. Saul has been counting his troops and the army was slipping away. Soon there will not be enough of an army left to put up a fight. Driven by fear and a lack of trust Saul chooses to have a man made worship service. Saul has asked God to get on board with his plan rather than waiting on God to act.

When Samuel arrives and hears what has transpired, he says, "You have done a foolish thing, You have not kept the command the LORD your God gave you; if you had, he would have established your kingdom over Israel for all time."

Saul's cancerous retreat from a loving God condemns the fruit of his loins. Any clarity he may once have had, any insight into God's desires, is being quickly replaced by his haunting fears. These fears will drive him to heinous ungodly actions. One of Saul's godless actions brings death to Uriah the Hittite's family and friends.

How often in today's world do Christians suffer mental and physical trauma due to the self seeking godless acts of another human being. Intoxicated drivers kill hundreds of innocent people every year in automobile accidents. Christians in the Middle East are beheaded for simply accepting Jesus Christ as their Savior. The greed of the money changer causes thousands to lose life-savings in dubious stock market schemes. The self-centered lies of highly contagious sick people infect others with deadly disease.

Our sin impacts others in fashions both seen and unseen. Our sin can ripple through times having unintended consequences long after our deaths. When sin caused events ripped apart Uriah the Hittite's life his eyes remained fixed on his Godly charge to be a "servant of servants." The simplest answer to overcoming injustice and unfairness in life is to focus on service to others. John 15:13 says, "Greater love hath no man than this, that a man lay down his life for his friends." (KJV)

In I Corinthians 13 the Apostle Paul shares when the terrible aspects of a fallen world rip into our lives Christians should not dwell in the offense. Christ provides every offended party the ability to bear up under terrible trials. Christ's love and charity never fails. And when the cares of worldly pressures and unfair treatment cause your understanding to become dark and clouded as if looking through a smoke stained and clouded window, remember that your faith, hope and love within your heart is greater than the world's pain roaring at your heart.

Chapter Eleven

When does one become a mighty man? When a King rejects placing faith in God...

King Saul is a product of his past. As shared in Smith's Bible Dictionary Saul's "character is in part illustrated by the fierce, wayward, fitful nature of the tribe. To this we must add a taint of madness which broke out in violent frenzy at times leaving him with long lucid intervals. He is remarkable for his strength and activity (2 Samuel 1:25) and, like the Homeric heroes, of gigantic stature, taller by head and shoulders than the rest of the people, and of that kind of beauty denoted by the Hebrew word "good," (1 Samuel 9:2) and which caused him to be compared to the gazelle, "the gazelle of Israel." (Smith's)

Saul is the "macho man" of his day. As his name denotes, he is desired by all. He is the rock star, football hero, basketball superstar and hunk of his generation. Saul suffered from the same proclivity that stardom visits on worldly heroes of this generation. The world showers praise on its heroes, and the heroes come to believe that they stand above those around them. Rules don't apply to those the world places on an alter. These stars sing to themselves a song of self adoration the lyrics of which epitomize a man's self-sufficiency and pride in living life their way without the first thought of humbling themselves before God.

Saul tastes a full measure of God's goodness. He tastes every gourmet dish on God's menu as he prophesied while descending the hill of God. Yet when Saul arrives home he stops prophesying. Saul stops with God's way and embraces his own way of doing things. When the adoring fans note that he is acting strangely, that is Godly, Saul will not speak the words of God.

Saul acts and says what Saul feels is right and just. Saul will not speak the words of one who kneels to an Almighty God.

God is the same yesterday, today and forever. There are no coincidences in his Word or actions through the centuries. In 1 Samuel 10:16 Samuel calls the people of Israel unto the Lord at the town of Mizpeh for the anointing of the king. Mizpeh is the town mentioned in Judges 20 and in Chapter Seven of this book. Mizpeh is the location where the children of Israel gather to do battle with the Tribe of Benjamin for the heinous acts perpetrated on the Levite's wife by the sons of Belial. Mizpeh is but a stone's throw from Saul's home town of Gibeah and his ancestral home of the sodomite sons of Belial.

Saul's first act following his public anointing as the nation of Israel's new king, is to look back and not forward. Saul chooses to "say the things he truly feels, and not the words of one who kneels" to God. Saul returns to the safety and comfort of his old ways. He returns to Gibeah his home as Samuel charged the nation to return home. But Saul does not retreat into seclusion to seek God's face. Saul does not fast as is asked of the nation during the last national convention at Mizpeh in 1 Samuel 7. Saul returns to the same old same old life.

Mark 10:29-31 records, "And Jesus answered and said, Verily I say unto you, There is no man that hath left house, or brethren, or sisters, or father, or mother, or wife, or children, or lands, for my sake, and the gospel's, But he shall receive an hundredfold now in this time, houses, and brethren, and sisters, and mothers, and children, and lands, with persecutions; and in the world to come eternal life. But many [that are] first shall be last; and the last first." (KJV)

Saul did not leave his house, or brethren, or father, or wife, or children. Saul returned to his old ways. Waiting for Saul when he arrived at his home in Gibeah are the children of Belial. These are the children of the sodomites that God had previously ordered completely destroyed. The children of Belial have a rebellious spirit cemented in their hearts. Saul returns to these children of Belial who are his family, friends and neighbors. These people had just witnessed one of their very own being named King by God. What is the response by these children of Belial? Saul's homecoming is one of taunts. The town of Gibeah cried out, "How shall this man save us? And they despised him, and brought him no presents."

Samuel's gathering of the nation in I Samuel 7 at Mizpeh is for a national cleansing and protection from the Philistine attack.

This is Saul's most recent example of a national referendum at Mitpeh. It is a call to holiness. This gathering brought the Ark of the Covenant to Kirjathjearim. The ark contained the shattered remains of the tablets on which God wrote the Ten Commandments. The revival meeting a Mizpeh focused on the first three of the Ten Commandments.

As written in Exodus 20:2-7 "I am the LORD thy God, which have brought thee out of the land of Egypt, out of the house of bondage. Thou shalt have no other gods before me. Thou shalt not make unto thee any graven image, or any likeness of any thing that is in heaven above, or that is in the earth beneath, or that is in the water under the earth: Thou shalt not bow down thyself to them, nor serve them: for I the LORD thy God am a jealous God, visiting the iniquity of the fathers upon the children unto the third and fourth [generation] of them that hate me; And shewing mercy unto thousands of them that love me, and keep my commandments. Thou shalt not take the name of the LORD thy God in vain; for the LORD will not hold him guiltless that taketh his name in vain." (KJV)

Saul had just experienced the wonder of the Spirit of God speaking through him as he prophesied coming down from the hill of God following Samuel's initial anointing. Saul's responsibility and accountability is found in 1 Samuel 10.7, "And let it be, when these signs are come unto thee, [that] thou do as occasion serve thee; for God [is] with thee." (KJV) Saul, rather than exercising faith, returns to his field and not to his knees.

Samuel at the Mizpeh meeting just prior to Saul's public anointing, told Israel told in 1Sa 7:3-8 "And Samuel spake unto all the house of Israel, saying, If ye do return unto the LORD with all your hearts, then put away the strange gods and Ashtoreth from among you, and prepare your hearts unto the LORD, and serve him only: and he will deliver you out of the hand of the Philistines. Then the children of Israel did put away Baalim and Ashtoreth, and served the LORD only. And Samuel said, Gather all Israel to Mizpeh, and I will pray for you unto the LORD. And they gathered together to Mizpeh, and drew water, and poured [it] out before the LORD, and fasted on that day, and said there, we have sinned against the LORD. And Samuel judged the children of Israel in Mizpeh. And when the Philistines heard that the children of Israel are gathered together to Mizpeh, the lords of the Philistines went up against Israel. And when the children of Israel heard it, they are afraid of the Philistines. And the children of Israel said to Samuel, Cease not to cry unto the LORD our God for us, that he will save us out of the hand of the Philistines." (KJV)

When Saul returns home not only is he insulted, but his friends and neighbors insult the God who has just established him king. Would not Saul's charge, "Do as occasion shall serve thee", cry for Saul to seek leadership and direction in dealing with those that blaspheme the God of Israel? Should Saul not react to this rebellion as the nation's leader when some of his people are acting in a fashion that can bring the entire nation into peril? Yet Saul walks away from the breaking of God's commandments by his friends and neighbors, the sons of Belial. Saul's first opportunity to lead a nation and continue to remove the scourge of Baalim and Ashtoreth is completely passed over.

Instead of looking forward to a clean fresh start with God, Saul looks back. The Jewish inhabitants of Jabesh-Gilead are threatened by the Ammonites. Word reaches Saul in Gibeah (on his way home from tending to the cattle in the field). Jabesh-Gilead is the town from which the eleven tribes sought brides for the Benjaminites that are not killed during the cleansing effort at Gibeah following the rape and murder by the men of Gibeah of the Levite's wife when their sexual desires for the Levite are thwarted.

The alliance between the surviving Benjaminites and Jabesh-Gilead is long standing. Saul interest in the well being of Jabesh-Gilead is immediately quickened. Jabesh-Gilead had not participated in the Benjaminite destruction and two-thirds of the Benjaminites descend from women of this community. A significant issue is that Jabesh-Gilead is not part of the Promised Land. The community lies east of the Jordan River in a territory given to the tribe of Gad, but Gad is one of the tribes that refused an inheritance within the Promised Land. Saul's first choice is to battle for the descendents of Gadites who had refused the Promised Land. Perhaps in an effort for Benjaminite payback Saul sends a message much like the message sent by the Levite that lead to the near eradication of his tribe. Saul does not dismember a dead women's body but he does dismember an oxen and sends pieces of the beast to the tribes to compel participation in a military operation outside the Promised Land.

King Saul's next major military operation is with the Amalekites. Chapter 15.3 of I Samuels opens with Samuel telling Saul of God desire for him to destroy the nation of Amalek and that not only are they to be utterly destroyed, but "you shall not have pity on Amalek; you shall slay both man and woman, infant and suckling, oxen, sheep, camel and ass." (KJV)

Amalek, as it was with Moses, represents the flesh. This is God's seeking to release Himself into Saul's and the nation's life through the destruction of fleshly reliance. God wants to redeem his people. A victory over Amalek is to picture the re-establishment of God's sovereignty over the mind and heart of a nation. A victory over Amalek is a gift given by God and not a victory won by an army. Saul only had 3000 soldiers at his first battle, yet he had amassed with his carved-up oxen threats over 200,000 men for this campaign against Amalek. It is one of the simplest tenets of the Christian faith, victory is not to be attained; victory is to be received as a gift from God. All that is required is to exercise the faith He has placed in your heart and follow His guidance until the victory is made real in your experience.

But Saul failed to understand that God saw nothing worth salvaging from Amalek. What is evil in Amalek is the energy of the flesh, and what is evil in Saul's victory over Amalek is it is achieved through the energy of the flesh. Saul believed that there is something good, something salvageable in his nature, but there is absolutely nothing good in practicing your religion through the energy of the flesh.

Saul's army vastly outnumbered Amalek. When Samuel is late in arriving Saul decides to start God's party without Him. Practicing your religion in the energy of the flesh often masquerades as God at work. With the numerically superiority of Saul's army, Saul triumphs. Saul had entered the battle without God and he exited the battle without God, yet He won the battle. Saul operating in the energy of the flesh decides he knows better than God. Saul is told to destroy everything in Amalek, bet he decides to keep alive Amalek's King Agag and the best of the sheep and cattle are taken as spoils of war. A battle with the flesh exercised by the flesh yields nothing worthy of keeping.

"Samuel approaches Saul and says, 'What is then this bleating of the sheep in my ears?' . . . And Saul answers, 'They the soldiers brought them from the Alamekites for the people had pity on the best of the sheep, and the oxen in order to sacrifice to the Lord, your God; and the rest we have utterly destroyed." (I Samuel 15:15) (KJV). God didn't want the filthy Amalek rags and yet through the eyes of the flesh Saul found value in not destroying everything. Saul justifies his fleshly actions by suggesting that he will dedicated his fleshly actions as a sacrifice to God.

When Samuel arrives he strikes down all of Saul's fleshly efforts. Samuel's prophetic words tell Saul he has behaved foolishly and the punishment for not having done the proper thing is that his kingdom will not continue forever. Samuel tells Saul that he is destined to lose his kingship.

King Saul will continue calling that which God has anointed as good bad. The practicing of a religion in the energy of the flesh does destroy good. This fleshly practice of religion on the part of Saul is what brought Uriah the Hittite into David's camp.

For what is a man? What has he got? Nothing!

God repeatedly shares that man has nothing He wants. The world's song says a man who does not control his own fate has nothing. A man must do what is right in his own eyes. A man must blurt out what he truly feels. A man is not a man if he kneels and does the bidding of others. Service somehow makes a man weak and less than a man. A man must take his blows and finish life's race, so when death knocks and the race ends he can proudly say I lived my life my way.

Uriah the Hittite through seeing friend and family murdered, through many years of physical hardship, through a cheating wife, through a despicable boss, and through becoming a living sacrifice lived his life God's way.

Chapter Twelve

When does Uriah become a mighty man? When Saul's cancer metastasizes...

King Saul slowly starts to become aware of the complete absence of God in his life. The Spirit of the Lord had come upon Saul as he visited the "hill of God" shortly following his anointing. Saul has experienced what God's will for his life could mean. Jehovah, the Great I Am, is the cure to all that ailed him and his brethren. The sinful stain that taints his tribe could be washed away and healed. The sin stain in Saul's life can be made clean. Everything available to God to open the door for Saul's entry into a life of faith has been made available to him through God's grace. But Saul is not a man of God's own choosing. Saul is a man of the people's choosing.

God is not pleased with the choice his chosen people were making. God has not raised up Saul for this task. God himself is King of Kings and Lord of Lords. The people do not listen to God through the message Samuel delivers, so God gives the people their heart's desire. God is nowhere to be found in the expression of that desire.

God tells Samuel to tell His people this course is not what he wants for them, yet the people clamor for an earth bound King with even greater fervor. God is not happy with the sin driven whining of His chosen people. But as often happens the potter finds it necessary to pick up the lump of clay and slam it down on the potter's wheel to work out imperfections, and God is just about ready to body slam an entire nation.

The New Living Bible shares God's intentions in Hosea 13:9-11, "You are about to be destroyed, O Israel—yes, by me, your only helper. Now where is your king? Let him save you! Where are all the leaders of the land, the king and the officials you demanded of me? In my anger I gave you kings, and in my fury I took them away." (NLV)

The children of Israel face a beating with a rod of their own choosing, so as a nation they can again learn how much better heavenly leadership is than that of this earth.

A modern parallel occurs with the father of a family of four children. The children grow up in the era of conversion vans which predates the mighty SUVs of today. The family is fond of taking long over the road vacations in the spaciousness of the large conversion van. The children each have a copious amount of space to reside and pass the time. The van's large windows provide panoramic views of the changing wonders found in God's countryside.

During the vacation a ruckus starts to break out among the children. Rather than enjoying what they did have in the wonders of the beautiful scenery, the children's focus turns inward to what their brother or sister had in their possession. Numerous warnings are issued from the driver's seat to enjoy the blessings they are missing while engaging in petty squabbling, but the children reject the repeating warnings.

Finally the father's indignation can no longer be restrained. The father hears one of his daughter's reignite the whining by saying to her brother, "Stop breathing my air!"

The conversion van pulls to the side of the road in a cloud of western prairie dust. The father exits the van and walks to the passenger side doors of the van. The father directs the horrified children to exit out of the van and line up alongside the vehicle. The father extracts from his trousers his pocket knife. The father opens the knife and hands it to his oldest son and points to a nearby small tree. The father directs the son to go to the tree and cut a switch with which each child will receive their just reward. The father's only admonition to his son is not to make him visit the tree if he returns with a switch that does not do justice to the reckless disregard of his many warnings.

As with this earthly father's vacation discipline in a conversion van so much more does God know how to bring glory to Himself from the rebellion of His children. God serves His own wise purposes even through the foolishness of His creations. With God there is never surprise at the foolish actions of his creations and no length to which He will not go to correct the course of those He has chosen.

Saul is given a full measure of God from which to drink, and he stops drinking. Edward Dorn Griffin in his sermon "Can These Dry Bones Live?" asks these challenging questions:

"Will you thus trifle with Him on whom your salvation depends? With so much at stake upon his will, dare you turn your backs on him and rush after idols? Will you refuse Him the homage of your prayers? Will you any longer provoke Him by your unbelief and sin? Will you violate His laws and assail His throne? And all this while He is looking on? All this while His will is to decide your eternal fate? Is it prudent thus to treat an almighty Sovereign who has you in His hands? Is it safe to rush thus upon the thick bosses of His buckler? What infatuation has seized thee, O presumptuous worm? Stay, stay thy mad career. Drop those weapons from your bloody hands. —Fall down at his feet. There say, I resign myself a prisoner into thy hands, to be disposed of as thou shalt see fit." (Sprague, 1839)

Saul is given specific instructions by God through Samuel regarding his military campaign aimed at the destruction on Amalek, God's sworn enemy. Yet Saul refuses to fall down at God's feet. Amalek is a picture of the human flesh, and Saul yields to the flesh. There is nothing good to be found in the fallen human flesh. There is no good decision that results from the flesh. God has given Saul specific instructions prior to the initiation of the destruction of Amalek. Wait on Samuel are God's orders. Samuel is of course God's earthly representative, so God is telling Saul to wait on God. But Saul, this presumptuous worm, thought God unnecessary save a token nod through his own machinating sham of a church service.

The cancer eating away at Saul which has been held at bay by God now metastasizes through Saul's choice not to expunge his reliance on his abilities. I Samuel 15 tells us Saul gets tired of waiting on Samuel. Saul performs his own little church service in the absence of Samuel, and then takes his forces to war against Amalek. Can you imagine an untrained patient attempting to self-perform a neurosurgeon's task of removing a cancerous brain tumor? Well, such a choice Saul makes. Saul doubles-down putting his nation and his family heritage on the line.

When Samuel arrives on the scene the battle has been won, and Saul's engorged pride is proud as punch. Saul boasts in Samuel 15.13, "Blessed be thou of the LORD: I have performed the commandment of the LORD." But the prophet Samuel will have none of it. Samuel's response is, "What meaneth then this bleating of the sheep in mine ears, and the lowing of the oxen which I hear?" (KJV) Saul has been ordered to destroy every living creature resident in Amalek. His army is to kill every man, women and child. No spoils are to be taken, so every sheep, cow, ox, dog, and cat, everything that took breath is to die.

The testimony of the farm animals convicted Saul of his hypocrisy. The boasting of a great victory for God comes crashing down by the bleating of a single sheep saved from the Amalek's destruction. Saul lies to himself and to God.

This biblical scene again plays out in the New Testament's story of Ananias and Sapphira in Acts chapters four and five. The Holy Spirit convicts many in the first century church to forgo the benefit of their personal property through an act of faith in God as Jehovah Jireh, the Lord will provide. The benefits from the sale of property by these early Christians are handed over to God for His disposal through the apostles to the less fortunate in the church. Yet Ananias and Sapphira, like Saul, do not give to God all that he has asked. Following Ananias's sale of his property he colludes with his wife Sapphira to withhold a portion of the sale. Ananias and Sapphira choose to worship God in the flesh by not giving God all of that which has been promised to God. Saul also refused to give God all that is asked of him.

In the New Testament story the apostle Peter calls out Ananias's sin, just as Samuel calls out Saul's sin. Acts 5.5 describes what happens to Ananias when he lies to God. "When Ananias heard this, he fell down and died. And great fear seized all who heard what had happened."

When Saul is called out by the prophet on his sin, he makes excuses, he starts the blame game. Matthew Henry shares in his commentary on 1 Samuel 15.14 that, "Sin is a brat that nobody cares to have laid at his doors. It is the sorry subterfuge of an impenitent heart, that will not confess its guilt, to lay the blame on those that were tempters, or partners, or only followers in it." (Henry)

Saul's impenitent heart has been weighted on God's balances and comes up way short. Samuel pronounces Saul's fate in 1 Samuel 15 22-23. "But Samuel replies: "Does the LORD delight in burnt offerings and sacrifices as much as in obeying the LORD? To obey is better than sacrifice, and to heed is better than the fat of rams. For rebellion is as the sin of witchcraft, And stubbornness is as iniquity and idolatry because you have rejected the word of the LORD, He also has rejected you from being king." (KJV)

Saul does not immediately die as did Ananias, but his death and his family's death will soon follow as did the death of Ananias's wife Sapphira. Saul flips God's commands on their heads. When God calls something bad his creatures ought not do an end run around God and pronounce it good. Yet this is Saul's testimony. Saul is kept alive and calls good that to which God prescribes destruction.

Saul's downward spiral will now be left completely unchecked. Saul's personal destruction and his destruction of the nation is full speed ahead. From Saul's growing hatred of God will spring Uriah the Hittite. Saul's actions regarding Uriah the Hittite and Uriah's people pronounce a death sentence on what remains of much Saul's family following his death.

Saul has already taken what God has pronounced as bad and called it good. Through the remainder of the time God allows Saul power in Israel, what God has pronounced as good Saul calls bad and seeks to destroy it.

As explored earlier Uriah the Hittite is almost certainly living in or near the city of Gibeon. His Gibeonite ancestors had gained their city's salvation from Joshua. Uriah's clan descended from Ham and Canaan, but as a clan they submitted to God's direction for their lives. They are ordered to live as "servants of servants" within God's proper order. The Gibeonites accepted their role and eventual became a group known as previously discussed the Nethinims, the given or dedicated ones. As a group they are given to the Levites to serve as carriers of wood and water especially for worship in the Tabernacle.

The Gibeonites are not of Hebrew heritage. Gibeonites were a gentile people adopted into God's family. As a group, the

Gibeonites perform their temple duties flawlessly over several hundred years. Through their faithful delivery of wood and water to the Tabernacle for the "sin offerings" of the Jewish people, again they were called the Nethinims.

Understanding the operation of Saul's sin twisted mind without the presence of God as a mitigating factor is evil run rampant. Satanic driven behavior oozes from Saul's every pore. It is not enough for Saul to slaughter Ahimelech and the Levite priests living in Nod for assisting in David's escape from his clutches. Yes, Saul actually lines up the preachers and has them hacked to death. His blood lust not satisfied Saul also murders much of the population found in Gibeon which is only a short distance from Nod. The Nethinims living in Gibeon are the people who had provide the servant's service for the Levites during worship. It is not difficult to image how Saul's blood curding hatred of God could be so easily redirected to the one group of people, a gentile people, the Nethinims, the Gibeonites, the Hittites, who had remained faithful to God's calling on their lives.

The genocidal atrocity visited on the Hittite descendents of Gibeon, the people who had provided Abraham a grave for Sarah, was left unpunished for many years. It was a nasty little event the nation would just rather not remember. But God remembers what men would rather forget.

The story of this senseless massacre is related in 2Sa 21:1-6:

"There is a famine during David's reign that lasted for three years, so David asked the LORD about it. And the LORD said, "The famine has come because Saul and his family are guilty of murdering the Gibeonites." (KJV) So King David summons the Gibeonites. The Gibeonites are not part of Israel but are adopted into the nation. The people of Israel have sworn not to kill them, but Saul, in his misguided hate filled zeal for Israel and Judah, attempts to wipe the Gibeonites out. David asked them, "What can I do for you? How can I make amends so that you will bless the LORD's people again? Well, money can't settle this matter between us and the family of Saul," the Gibeonites replied. "Neither can we demand the life of anyone in Israel. What can I do then?" David asked. "Just tell me and I will do it for you." Then they replied, "It is Saul who planned to destroy us, to keep us from having any place at all in the territory of Israel. So let seven of Saul's sons be handed over to us, and we will execute them before the LORD at Gibeon, on the mountain of the LORD." "All right," the king said, "I will do it." (NLV)

Survivors did escape the savage violence visited upon Gibeon. Uriah the Hittite is most assuredly one of those survivors. Uriah, given his working relationship with the tabernacle and the Levites, would have been aware of the nature of the battle between David and Saul. Uriah would have known of Samuel's anointing of David as King and Saul's repudiation. The resulting intrigue is visited upon Uriah's life when his friends and family die beneath Saul's bloody sword at Gibeon. The shame of Saul's murderous actions is manifested in God's bringing a just resolution to this grievance through execution of Saul's sons and grandsons. Saul's sin is visited on a second and third generation.

And Uriah the Hittite, the resident of Gibeon, the wood and water carrier in the tabernacle is made a refugee of genocide against his people.

The Uriah the Hittite's traumatic experience as he witnesses the murdering of the Gibeonite people, the complete loss of his home and belongings, the unspeakable horror visited on the women by King Saul's soldiers, his complete uprooting and suffering drives him. Yet the stability of Uriah's long established service to God through the carrying of wood and water at the tabernacle needs to be maintained. Into the service of God's anointed leader is the only place Uriah the Hittite can go to maintain the "servant of servants" calling on his life.

Chapter Thirteen

Where does Uriah go to become a mighty man? When he enters David's camp...

Rather than fight King Saul, David retreats. He retreats and fortifies his band in a cave near the town of Adullam. The town of Adullam lies in territory allotted to the Tribe of Judah. It seems little wonder that David would retreat to a town whose name translates to "the justice of the people". For the justice is found in the righteousness of the people. It is not the people's righteousness but the righteousness of the God whom they follow.

1Sa 22:1-2 says, "David therefore departed thence, and escaped to the cave Adullam: and when his brethren and all his father's house heard it, they went down thither to him. And every one that is in distress, and every one that is in debt, and every one that is discontented, gathered themselves unto him; and he became a captain over them: and there were with him about four hundred men."

David is anointed of God, and he separates himself from the worldly reign of King Saul. David's separation from the worldly reign of King Saul provides those a clear choice. David, like Christ, is now rejected by man and received by God. There is now no neutrality in Switzerland. Men and women must now choose to follow Christ or follow the world.

In chapter seven a passage from Major Ian Thomas's great work The Mystery of Godliness is quoted and it is again here appropriate.

"The moment you come to realize that only God can make a man godly, you are left with no option, but to find God, and to know

God, and to let God be God in you and through you, whoever He may be-and this will leave you no margin for picking and choosing- for there is only one God, and He is absolute, and He made you expressly for Himself!" (Thomas, 1964)

So into the town of "the justice of the people" came all those who are distressed, who have debt they cannot pay, or people who are discontent. The crowd comes looking for righteousness. They accept the branding of being the outcasts of the world. 400 come to the cave to join David. The 400 in the cave make a choice for God and against the world of King Saul.

The reference Jesus uses in Matthew chapter seven is striking when one actually sees the Cave of Adullam. Inside the cave is security and safety. The location is abundantly supplied with water and provides a fortified camp. From the advantage of mouth of the cave no enemy can surprise those that dwell within. The entrance to the cave is securely guarded by steep heights funneling all who would enter onto a narrow path.

Mathew records Jesus saying in chapter seven verses thirteen and fourteen of his gospel 7:13-14, "Enter ye in at the strait gate: for wide is the gate, and broad is the way, that leadeth to destruction, and many there be which go in there at: Because strait is the gate, and narrow is the way, which leadeth unto life, and few there be that find it."

David and his small band take refuge in the Most High and that refuge and fortress is later revealed as Jesus Christ. Redemption is found through that narrow gate into the life giving and life sustaining grace of Our Lord Jesus Christ. Rejected by the world that chooses Saul to be their king, those resting in security of the Cave of Adullam identify themselves with Christ, they are the redeemed.

In another of his magnificent books, <u>The Saving Life of Christ</u>, Major Ian Thomas says, "To be in Christ- that is redemption: but for Christ to be in you- that is sanctification! To be in Christ- that makes you fit for heaven: but for Christ to be in you- that makes you fit for earth! To be in Christ- that changes your destination- but for Christ to be in you- that changes your destiny! The one makes heaven your home- the other makes this world His workshop." (Thomas 1961)

David and his band reside in a humble place totally in the care and protect of the Good Shepherd. But sheep reside in the fold when the Good Sheppard places them in the fold for their safety and protection. When the gate of the fold opens the sheep follow the Good Shepherd out into the world and overcome the world.

Peter says in I Peter 5.6, "Humble yourselves, therefore, under the mighty hand of God, that He may exalt you at the proper time..." When this motley band exits the Cave of Adullam they change their destiny, Israel's destiny, the world's destiny, and yes your and my destiny. And it is here with David in the Cave of Adullam Uriah the Hittite is found.

For who is it that is found in this cave with David, it is "everyone who is in distress, and everyone who is in debt, and everyone who is discontented, gathered to him; and he became captain over them." Uriah the Hittite is most likely a refugee from the genocide at Gibeon, he may have even watched as King Saul slaughters the priest and Levites at Nob who served the tabernacle where he worked as a Nethinim. Yes, Uriah the Hittite is amongst the distressed, the debtors and the discontented who gather in the Cave of Adullam.

The nature of those called by God has not changed through the centuries. Paul in his letter to the Corinthians says in chapter 1 verse 26, "For ye see your calling, brethren, how that not many wise men after the flesh, not many mighty, not many noble, are called: But God hath chosen the foolish things of the world to confound the wise; and God hath chosen the weak things of the world to confound the things which are mighty; And base things of the world, and things which are despised, hath God chosen, yea, and things which are not, to bring to nought things that are: That no flesh should glory in his presence." (KJV)

The words distress, debt and discontent don't really carry in today's language the same level of pain exacted in the Cave of Adullam. Distress in the Cave of Adullam describes the willingness that could overwhelm a mother starving in a city under siege who is pressed by hunger pangs into a willingness to eat the flesh of her own child. How many mothers today know this angst of soul, of this level of distress, after sacrificing the life of an unborn child at an abortion clinic to another lust of the flesh? How many need the rest and refuge found in the Cave of Adullam to quiet their soul's pain?

Those in the Cave of Adullam may be in debt quite possible due to lost employment. Their employer may have poorly managed the business and through no fault of their own, the former employee suffers under the threat of incredibly harsh sanctions. In that day those in debt faced more than a trip to bankruptcy court and a few years of a rotten credit rating. The debtor could be thrown into prison and families could be sold into slavery to satisfy the claims of the money changers. Victor Hugo's Les Miserables' character Jean Valjean knew this pressure well when Valjean says' "If I speak, I am condemned. If I stay silent, I am damned!"

This separation from the world is not of some monk calling for self-flagellation. Everyone in Israel knows that God through his agent Samuel has anointed David to be King over the nation. David is God's choice; Saul had won the people's choice award. Many ate at Saul's table, even Jonathan who had sworn a covenant with David in 1 Samuel 18.3-3, "Then Jonathan and

David made a covenant, because he loved him as his own soul. And Jonathan stripped himself of the robe that is upon him, and gave it to David, and his garments, even to his sword, and to his bow, and to his girdle." (KJV)

Matthew Henry shares in his commentaries on 1 Samuel 18, "David is seen in Jonathan's clothes, that all may take notice he is a Jonathan's second self. Our Lord Jesus has thus shown his love to us, that he stripped himself to clothe us, emptied himself to enrich us; nay, he did more than Jonathan, he clothed himself with our rags, whereas Jonathan did not put on David's." (Henry) Jonathan is an Old Testament picture of the New Testament's rich young ruler. Jonathan wanted David in his world, but he was not willing to give up his world to enter David's world.

Those who entered the Cave of Adullam make the decision to follow God's anointed. Matthew 7.14 says, "Because strait is the gate, and narrow is the way, which leadeth unto life, and few there be that find it." (KJV) The four hundred in the cave had more than an emotional or intellectual understanding. The four hundred that number Uriah the Hittite as a member act on the conviction God places in their hearts. These four hundred are not redeemed and sanctified by withdrawing from the world and the problems that pursued them. It is the four hundred's entry through that narrow path that sets them apart from Jonathan. These four hundred are joining God's army not David's army. They know that God accepts them as they are in spite of their inadequacies and past failures. God places in their hearts a faith and strength that supplants human weakness. They trade their personal failure for a divine victory. The distress, debt and discontent of their bankrupt souls is exchanged for a future limited only by an unlimited God.

Within the four hundred in the Cave of Adullam are found other of David's mighty men. The unlimited nature of God's strength exhibited through these men of faith is extraordinary. David relates in a codicil to his last will and testament in 2 Samuel 23 the stories God's inspiration through many of these men. One of the top three in this record by David is Adino. Adino slew 800 enemy soldiers at one time with only his spear. Then there is Eleazar who taunts a large Philistine army much like Goliath of Gath perpetrated on King Saul and the Israel's army. The Philistines attack and many that stand with Eleazar run from the fight. Eleazar holds his ground and then chases down the remaining Philistines as they attempted to flee the battle. Eleazar's hand is so fused to his sword that when the fighting ends he is unable break his hand free of the sword.

Once when my children were young we visited a famous theme park in central Florida during a spring break. Our children fought fatigue until the very end. We remained at the park until the last parade was complete and the last firework fades from the night sky. The campground where we lodged was a long boat ride and walk from the main theme park. One of my sons collapses into a deep sleep prior to our passing the park exit, but not before asking his father to carry him. Once the 50 pounder is in my arm, he slumps his head over my shoulder and is out like a light. When I place him in his bed over an hour later I came to the sudden realization that I could not straighten my arm. It had become fused in the position that I held my son. I can only imagine Eleazar's struggles to remove a fatigued hand from a sword when the hand had been empowered by the Holy Spirit. Who knows, it may have taken days for the hand to release the sword. When Moses descended from Mt. Sinai God's glory remained shining on his face for days.

With the slightest of fanfare Uriah the Hittite is the very last mighty man to be mentioned in David's will. The greatest act of service by any of David's mighty men is performed by Uriah the Hittite, and it seems the guilt carried by David may have nearly suppressed the awarding of any honor, or in the end perhaps

David never truly understood the nature of Uriah the Hittite's sacrifice.

Earlier in the chapter a quote from Matthew Henry's commentary noted that Jonathan, King Saul's son, dressed David in his princely garments, but Jonathan did not reciprocate. Jonathan did not dress himself in David's ragged, filthy smelly sheep herder clothing. Jonathan for all the sincerity of his covenant with David never joined him in the Cave of Adullam. Jonathan never pushed himself away from his earthly father's table.

Uriah the Hittite did put on the filthy rags of King David. Uriah the Hittite knowingly covered himself in the filthy rags of King David's horrific sin. Uriah the Hittite dies in place of his King. Uriah the Hittite, the Nethinim, the servant of servants from his years carrying wood and water to the bronze laver and alter fire in the tabernacle knows the meaning of a sin offering. Uriah the Hittite knows only the blood of a sin offering can cover the stain of King David's sin. Uriah the Hittite makes himself that sin offering when King David has lost his way. The first shall be last and the last shall be first. Of all King David's mighty men, Uriah the Hittite is first on God's list. John 15:13 says, "Greater love hath no man than this, that a man lay down his life for his friends." (KJV) Uriah the Hittite's service to his king will mean forfeiting his own life, even when Uriah is last on the king's list.

Chapter Fourteen

When does Uriah become a mighty man? A man who knows God supplies...

Uriah the Hittite entered the Cave of Adullam numbered among "everyone who was in distress, and everyone who was in debt, and everyone who was discontented, gathered to him; and he became captain over them." Uriah the Hittite is a refugee from the genocide at Gibeon. Uriah the Hittite may have witnessed King Saul's slaughtering of the priest and Levites at Nob who served the tabernacle. Yes, Uriah the Hittite was amongst the distressed, the debtors and the discontent who gather in the Cave of Adullam. Uriah exits the Cave of Adullam a member of David's small army.

The Israelites are a people whose history is wrought with warfare, but the warfare always has a purpose. The battle is that of God's, and the victory is God's provision. Even in defeat God has a purpose for his people. So in victory or defeat everyone who is in distress, and everyone who is in debt, and everyone who is discontent should gather to God; and let God be captain over them.

This is a fairly motley crew who gather in the Cave of Adullam, but the small army does muster the faith to exit the cave with their new leader. These men enter the cave subjects of King Saul and the men exit the immersion of the cave subjects of a new king. These men look to establish a new kingdom in Israel. These are men looking forward and not looking to that which is behind them. Comfort and solace lay before them. It is a young army looking to God's newly anointed King for leadership.

But as with any new endeavor established by God, testing is always incorporated. The test is always about faith. Is God our

Father in control or is He not in control? Regardless of circumstance are the faithful servants willing to trust their God despite what is seen immediately in front of their faces? Do circumstances control the faithful or does faith in God control the faithful?

This small army through the faith God places in their hearts enters the Cave of Adullam. It is a picture of the justification God provides through the narrow way provided by His Son Jesus Christ. As the small band of warriors exited the cave the picture of sanctification begins. Sanctification is also a narrow path through the world. Ephesians 2:10 "For we are his workmanship, created in Christ Jesus unto good works, which God hath before ordained that we should walk in them." There is good work God has specifically designed for each Christian to do. One must be tuned into God and hear him speaking those acts to us through the Holy Spirit. It is a narrow personal path for each Christian, but the instructions are simple. Hear God, and do what God says.

This struggle between faith and circumstance is at the root of all sin. In the Bible's first Book of Genesis we find Adam. Adam remained untarnished by sin, and he cared for Eden an untold number of years. Adam lived in perfect harmony with his Creator. Adam exercised a true and undefiled faith every day of his life right up to The Fall. A loving Creator and Father had but two tasks He asked of Adam. The first job is a very simple request and warning. The task requires absolutely no effort on the part of Adam to accomplish save obedience. Absolutely no drop of sweat is required Adam or any need to dry his brow. Adam was simply asked not to eat of the one thing in the Garden of Eden that would kill him. "Adam," God said, "don't eat the "rat poison". If you eat the rat poison it will kill you. Genesis 2:16-17 says, "And the LORD God commanded the man, saying, Of every tree of the garden thou mayest freely eat: But of the tree of the knowledge of good and evil, thou shalt not eat of it:

for in the day that thou eatest thereof thou shalt surely die." (KJV)

When Adam ate the "rat poison" of the tree of the knowledge of good and evil, he consumes the knowledge of good and evil. When eating of the fruit Adam chooses to act outside the will of God. Adam performs his first faithless act, the act of acting on his own. Adam changes the verses in the Lord's Pray. Matthew 6:9-13 records Jesus' words on how to pray, "After this manner therefore pray ye: Our Father which art in heaven, Hallowed be thy name. Thy kingdom come. Thy will be done in earth, as it is in heaven. Give us this day our daily bread. And forgive us our debts, as we forgive our debtors. And lead us not into temptation, but deliver us from evil: For thine is the kingdom, and the power, and the glory, for ever. Amen."

In effect Adam rewrites this prayer when he chooses to turn a faithless back to his Creator and God. Adam prays I am equal to the Father in heaven in deciding what is best for me, what is right and wrong for me and what is good and evil for me, hallowed be the name of Adam. My kingdom will be as I decide. My will be done in earth, and God can do what He wants in heaven. I will make my way in this world. I will make decisions based on what is best for me and owe no man anything yet every other man owes me everything. I need not be delivered from temptation and evil because I decide what is good and evil in my own eyes. It is my house, my strength and ability, my magnificence and splendor, my opinion, judgment and understanding that will endure forever. Adam and Adam

What makes Jesus the perfect sacrifice is not what He did as God, but what he did as a man. Unlike Adam who chooses to act like God, Jesus while walking this world as a man always acts as a man and never as God. Jesus' earthly perfection, what made him the perfect sacrifice, is that He lived a perfect life as a man.

How is it that He lived that perfect life you might ask? As a man He never ate from the "tree of the knowledge of good and evil." Jesus never acted as God while living as man. His dependence is always 100 percent on his Father. Jesus lives a life of faith while he walks the earth. Jesus listens to His Father and executes God the Father's plan for His life on the earth. Jesus always does and only does what his Father tells him to do. Jesus never exercises His will as the Son of God while He walks this earth, but relies totally on His Father to direct his steps. Jesus thus offers to God the Father a perfect life lived as man. Again, Jesus always and only did what God the Father told him to do. Jesus never ate of the tree of the knowledge of good and evil for Jesus always serves the will of His Father and never His own will as a man.

Jesus passes the test of life. He never questions His Father's decisions. There are many who fall prey to a theology that suggests Jesus in Gethsemane was praying a prayer to His Father in heaven to relieve Him from the savage death that lies before Him. Luke 22:42 records, "Saying, Father, if thou be willing, remove this cup from me: nevertheless not my will, but thine, be done." (KJV)

Is Jesus kibitzing? Is He praying for a way out of the horrific death He was about to die? If Jesus would have prayed a pray in His own will, He would have acted in a fallen man's nature. He would have decided what was good and what was bad as a man. He would have asked His Father in heaven to provide Him a way out of the perfect plan of salvation; a plan orchestrated by God the Father. Had Jesus prayed such a prayer He would have sinned. Jesus would have had spot and blemish on his record, and His life would have been an unacceptable sacrifice.

Jesus' prayer in Gethsemane is answered. Jesus is the Lion of Judah. To suggest that this warrior, a man who has prepared for this battle for 33 years, would at the last minute harbor a thought of running away, well who would want a whimpering man to call

Savior? There are literally thousands of men who have faced battle without prayerfully muttering selfish desires. So what was Jesus praying about in Gethsemane?

The cup of which Jesus speaks is the dregs of sin and death. Jesus knew that once He put on the sin of the world that God the Father would not be able to look upon him. God turns His back on His Son as testified to by Jesus' cry of being forsaken on the cross. But once the sin of the world had been put on by Christ and His perfect life is accepted by His Father in exchange for man's sin, Jesus' prayer in Mat 26:39, "And he went a little further, and fell on his face, and prayed, saying, O my Father, if it be possible, let this cup pass from me: nevertheless not as I will, but as thou wilt." (KJV) was affirmatively answered. God the Father returned to His Son and the cup of sin and death passed from His Son. The price was paid in full for the sin of the world, the perfect exchange.

So tests come to all who choose Christ, and it is no different for this young army of David. In 1 Samuel 27 we see a young king waiver under the pressure of leadership and faith in God. The test God prepares for David is far greater than facing a bear, lion of even Goliath.

King Saul's heart is hardened much like the Pharaoh's heart is hardened when Moses departs Egypt with the children of Israel. No matter the devastation that visits Egypt, Pharaoh's pride cannot bring him to allow the disgrace of defeat at the hands of God working through Moses. The children of Israel are pursued by the Egyptians. In one last miraculous act the pursuing Egyptian army follows God's children into the Red Sea and the sea swallowed up and washed away Pharaoh's would be last attack.

King Saul's life is twice put in peril by David. David first shows King Saul mercy when King Saul hunts David and his men in

En-gedi. En-gedi is an oasis on the western shore of the Dead Sea. En-gedi translates to "the fountain or spring of young goats". It is the only source of fresh water for miles in an arid region. What an image of God as this newborn army walks the narrow path of sanctification! David's eyes could see miles of lifeless water at this oasis on the Dead Sea, but only this one fountain following out of the desert provides him and his men with the water of life.

David and his men's peaceful refuge is suddenly interrupted by the arrival of King Saul and his army at En-gedi. David and his men hid in the coolness of one of the caves near the spring. In an act of God's providential hand, King Saul also takes refuge for a siesta from the hot desert sun in the exact same cave in which David and his men are hidden. David's men encourage David to kill King Saul, but as Uriah the Hittite looks on David refused to lay a hand on him who God anointed King. David said I "will not put forth my hand against my lord, for he is God's anointed." David's words reverberated in Uriah the Hittite's soul.

Uriah the Hittite watches David stealthfully humiliate King Saul by cutting away a piece of King Saul's garment. It was for David a misbegotten act of vengeance extracted from his pursuer. David's message to King Saul is you are as a dead man.

K'riah is a Jewish funeral tradition. The rending or tearing off a piece of a decedent's garment by mourners symbolizes the death of the outer garment, a person's physical body. K'riah is for the mourners to express the true feelings within their hearts for the departed soul.

But King Saul did not need to have David deliver such a morbid and demeaning message. God was sharing with David and his men that He could put an end to King Saul's pursuit anytime that He wanted. David, on the other hand, was sending King Saul the message I could have killed you. Matthew 5:28 says, "But I say unto you, That whosoever looketh on a woman to lust after her hath committed adultery with her already in his heart." (KJV) Rewriting the verse to cover another forbidden act in the Ten Commandments this verse could easily say, "But I say unto you, That whosoever looketh on a man to kill him hath already killed him in his heart." A little further on in the same fifth chapter of Matthew verses 38-39 Christ says, "Ye have heard that it hath been said, An eye for an eye, and a tooth for a tooth: But I say unto you, That ye resist not evil: but whosoever shall smite thee on thy right cheek, turn to him the other also." (KJV)

Uriah the Hittite may have been the only warrior present in the cave who hears God's message of "I've got your back" and believes it.

In 1 Samuel 24.5 David is immediately convicted of his affront to God's anointed and the black motive in his heart. The verse states, "And it came to pass afterward, that David's heart smote him, because he had cut off Saul's skirt." (KJV) David is convicted for cutting away King Saul's garment for David fails to view the event with the eyes of faith. David initially misses God's message of protection and follows his own course, and then he simply refuses to obey. David turns a deaf ear to the still small voice whispering to him stop, don't cut that garment. I've got your back.

David continues his affront to King Saul's dignity by calling King Saul out after King Saul departs the cave. God has no need of letting King Saul know David and his men were in the cave where he had just napped. God put King Saul to sleep so he will not be made aware of David's presence. God has already delivered judgment on King Saul and his house, and it was within God's grasp to finish King Saul's reign anytime He so desired. God certainly didn't need David reinforcing the message to King Saul with the tawdry playing out of a funeral rite.

In 1 Samuel 24:10-12 David in all his piety speaks a self-fulfilling prophecy that again fell upon the ears of Uriah the Hittite, "Behold, this day thine eyes have seen how that the LORD had delivered thee to day into mine hand in the cave: and some bade me kill thee: but mine eye spared thee; and I said, I will not put forth mine hand against my lord; for he is the LORD'S anointed. Moreover, my father, see, yea, see the skirt of thy robe in my hand: for in that I cut off the skirt of thy robe, and killed thee not, know thou and see that there is neither evil nor transgression in mine hand, and I have not sinned against thee; yet thou huntest my soul to take it. The LORD judge between me and thee, and the LORD avenge me of thee: but mine hand shall not be upon thee." (KJV)

Uriah the Hittite witnesses David disregard the conviction God has placed on his heart. Uriah the Hittite through his service as a wood and water carrier in the temple understands the conviction David feels following the dishonorable act of cutting the King's garment. Uriah witnesses David forget his position and his failure to maintain the rightful order God establishes. David bites the fruit of the tree of the knowledge of good and evil. David decides for himself what the best course is given the current circumstances. David speaks words to King Saul at En-gedi that will be strangely prophetic as those words fall on Uriah the Hittite's ears.

In David's second effort "to put the fear of God" into King Saul, God did not choreograph the meeting. Rather, David acting out of his own initiative sends out spies to find King Saul and his army. Out of the presumption of God's protection based on the discarded conviction from his first affront to King Saul's position, David chooses to brazenly enter King Saul's camp at night.

How easily men find it to interpret God's protection as a confirmation of their own selfish actions when their decisions place them in harm's way and prompt their need for Godly intervention. Confusing God's grace and mercy when He protects us in our own foolishness should never be doubled down on as God's confirmation and approval of our folly.

David's only plan was to go down go down to King Saul's camp and pay him a visit. David takes with him his nephew Abishai and heads down to the camp in the middle of the night. One wonders what David had in mind. Did, like Navy Seals, the men creep up to the camp in the cover of darkness? The pair could have been nothing but stunned by what they found.

A deep sleep has fallen upon every member of King Saul's camp. The sentries whose lives hang in the balance for sleeping on their watch are unable to resist the deep slumber. David and Abishai are able to walk through the entire army and stand beside King Saul's bed looking down at his head. Next to King Saul's pillow is a glass of water and his spear. David and Abishai have a discussion at the head of King Saul's bed whether they should use his spear to finish King Saul's reign.

Humorist Will Rogers was famous for his wit and wisdom. Rogers' once quipped, "If I sleep with a gun under my pillow, I don't want somebody from across the street to 'advise' me that I don't need it." Yet King Saul and all in his camp are in such a deep sleep that David pulls off exactly what Will Rogers' humors. David and Abishai leave King Saul's camp with the "gun under his pillow", that is King Saul's spear and the glass of water King Saul has next to his pillow.

David works his way up a hill next to King Saul's camp and shouts down at the camp. David is that "somebody from across the street" advising King Saul that he doesn't need that spear next to his pillow or the glass of water from which to drink. King

Saul has someone right next to him as he sleeps. King Saul's life has been held in the balance. It is quite the message to King Saul who discontinues his hunt for David and his men.

Unfortunately God's mercy in protecting David through these impetuous acts did not build David's faith. The dishonoring of King Saul not once but twice brought no strength or courage to David's heart, only an unrelenting fear that King Saul would again return to hunt him and his men. The pervasive nature of this fear in David's heart is the weakness that undermines his faith. God will not employ actions which He has expressly forbidden to make His point.

David knows the commandments God delivered to Moses, yet David violates one of God's commandments to make his point to King Saul. David steals King Saul's spear and water cup. David delivers a like message through the theft of King Saul's bedside belongings. Unfortunately God is not the author of David's actions. 1Corinthians 14:33 states, "For God is not the author of confusion, but of peace, as in all churches of the saints." (KJV)

Confusion instead falls on David's mind through the seeds he has planted. In I Samuel 27.1 David says, "I shall now perish one day by the hand of Saul: there is nothing better for me than that I should speedily escape into the land of the Philistines; and Saul shall despair of me, to seek me any more in any coast of Israel: so shall I escape out of his hand." (KJV) So, David took all his men and their families and sought sanctuary from the Philistine Achish, the son of Maoch, King of Gath." David goes to an enemy of his God for protection because he does not believe God will protect him and his men from King Saul.

These names associated with David's new benefactor give insight into His character. Achish means 'I will terrify". Maoch means oppression. Gath is the name of the trough in which grapes are stomped until the pomace yields all its juice. So David sought aid from a fellow named 'I will terrify' who is the son of a fellow named "oppression" while living in a country named after the tool used to stomp the essence out of a grape and leaving behind only the skins.

David deserts Judah and seeks safety as servant to a descendant of Canaan. That which God calls bad David has decided to call good. At this point David's fear, his lack of faith in God's protection, brings him to dwell in the cesspool that is Gath. David is not unlike the prodigal son at this point in his life.

David is forced to equivocate if not outright lie to gain favor with Gath's King Achish. The fear driving David to dishonor King Saul is the same fear with which he dishonors himself when seeking refuge in Gath. David, in his first two major challenges on the narrow road of sanctification, yields to his fears as did Adam when he takes his eyes off his Father.

A test of faith builds faith. Once a student passes a test additional material is added and the knowledge base expands. Then along comes another test that measures how well the student has incorporated the influx of new knowledge and experience. David turns a blind eye to God's correction and conviction following the Cave at Adullam. David does not understand God is telling him that he has nothing to fear from King Saul. David has no peace from this fear of King Saul. David a second time tries to quash his own fears by sneaking into King Saul's camp and stealing his spear and water glass, but still there is no peace.

David misses the essence of God's protection twice! Twice God had put King Saul asleep in his presence and twice David found it necessary to kick the sleeping dog. The meaning of the idiom, "Let sleeping dogs lie" flies in one ear and out the other ear of David. David gains nothing by his actions other than fueling the fear that burns in his heart.

God looks into men's hearts and desires to build a new foundation from the bottom up. To that point in David's life God has always given David peace when He empowers him to action. David's victories over lions, bears and giants make him famous. David starts to believe his own press releases rather than listening to the God's voice. David starts acting religiously rather than depending on his relationship with God.

God looks at the tremendous turmoil in our lives; He sees the wind blowing waves to monstrous heights; and He sees those waves crashing down around His children. God's answer is not to give the waves a good threatening like a schoolyard bully. God says, "Peace be still." Psalms 46:10 says, "Be still, and know that I am God: I will be exalted among the heathen, I will be exalted in the earth." (KJV)

God did not need David's help to be exalted in heaven and earth. In the stillness and peace of King Saul's slumber David failed to be still. The God who grows the balm of Gilead from the life giving waters flowing from En-gedi's spring waters will also apply that balm to David's heart in the En-gedi cave. David hears God's conviction but shrugs off that conviction. Be still God shares with David. God says know and understand my protection, but David does neither.

Through all of these events Uriah the Hittite watches his leader David. Uriah the Hittite recognizes and learns the weaknesses as well as the strengths of his new young King. Uriah the Hittite understands these trials to be tests of faith and remains faithful to his role as a "servant of servants". Uriah recognizes that God has David's back even though David fails to realize that fact.

We often see acquaintances struggle with sin issues in their lives. Our answer is often to act as David acted. The tendency is to get into the offender's face and provide them our explanation of what God has to say about their sinful endeavors. What would ever make a man think his words are equal to God and more powerful than God's words for the conviction of sin? Our answer is to pray for those that despitefully use us and not condemn their action with our interpretation of what God is doing in their lives.

Chapter Fifteen

What does Uriah become as mighty man? A man with a band of brothers...

Following David and his band of distressed, discontented paupers' departure from the Cave of Adullam, warfare followed these mighty men. The archeological and theological record is unclear for exactly how many years these men are constantly spilling the blood of the nation's enemies. Some theologians tally the number of years of continuous war for David and his mighty men at as few as 9 years while others will double that number to 18 years.

In recent years there have been several cinematic efforts that attempt to capture the essence of a military unit's esprit de corps. These men live, eat and sleep together as a military unit. Bonds arise between men-at-arms when they enter battle together. These bonds can be so strong that one man will willingly forfeit his life so a fellow comrade survives.

After a decade or more on the battlefield these 37 mighty men of King David shared the intimacy of a thousand camp fires. These battle harden leaders have developed into a cohesive group based on the bonding between superior and subordinate. These soldiers know their King with whom they live and fight, and to a man they are willingly to lay down their lives for him. King David's personal strengths and weakness cannot be hidden from these men. The stress of the battlefield strips bare a soldier's character for all his brothers to see.

The thousand campfires also present the opportunity for these mighty men to bond as peers. They are the elite warriors of their King's army, a Navy Seal unit might compare. The social relationships that develop between men who have looked deeply into each other's hearts are deeply held. These soldiers know a trust that only comes from being "all in" when trusting your back to another on the battlefield can cost you your life. These soldiers on those long nights away from home will share their personal lives. The one significant difference between these mighty men and a modern day military unit is they all started together in the Cave of Adullam. Many of these soldiers have their families traveling with the army. After 9 to 18 years of close quarters living these 37 men have watched each other marry, have children, and have seen their children marry.

There were no secrets in a community such as this. The spousal spats would have been known to all. An ill-behaving child would have been as obvious as the screaming unruly child struggling with parents during a night out at the local restaurant. A daughter radiant with physical beauty would not remain without the notice of eligible bachelors or admiring fathers who are considering arranging a marriage for a son. Exceptional offspring rarely go unnoticed.

Individual failings of those within King's David army also did not go unnoticed. In I Samuel 29 King David is about to wage war with the Philistine King Achish against King Saul's army. Divine providence intercedes on the behalf of David's army of six hundred, and they are ordered to depart. It is a three day march for King David's army to return to the town of Ziklag which had been given to David and his men by King Achish as a safe residence for their families.

But the safety and security promised by Satan's right hand man King Achish is no safety and security at all. Ziklag is a town whose name roughly translates 'winding' according to Strong's Exhaustive Concordance. One would expect from the devious twisted serpentine nature of Satan that his pocket man King Achish would offer a sinuous coiled snake of a gift that is waiting to provide a torturing surprise.

The three day march ends with the downward spiral of crushed family reunions. As King David's army neared their city of refuge there is smoke rising on the horizon. Many maps of the ancient Holy Lands place Ziklag on the coastal plain. The smoke is probably visible for miles. As the realization settles into their minds that the plumes of smoke on the horizon are their burning homes, the men would have started to run. One mile, five miles perhaps ten miles the men ran after a three day grueling march.

What followed is described in I Samuel 30.1-4, "And it came to pass, when David and his men were come to Ziklag on the third day, that the Amalekites had invaded the south, and Ziklag, and smitten Ziklag, and burned it with fire; And had taken the women captives, that were therein: they slew not any, either great or small, but carried them away, and went on their way. So David and his men came to the city, and, behold, it was burned with fire; and their wives, and their sons, and their daughters, were taken captives. Then David and the people that were with him lifted up their voice and wept, until they had no more power to weep." (KJV)

These soldiers are physically and emotional spent. There city is plundered and burned to the ground. Every wife, son and daughter is carried off. They pour out the grief in their hearts until not one tear is left in their eyes.

These trained soldiers recognize the signs the attackers leave behind. The destroyers of their city are the Amalekites. Their grief couple with their thoughts of Amalekite revenge overwhelmed them. Only a few short months have passed since King David led these men on a slaughter of Amalekite towns prior to seeking aid from the King of Gath. David's men killed men, women, children and infants. It was only a short jump for these exhausted men to start speculation on a cause and effect nature of these events. Had King David allowed us to stay at home, had King David not had us slaughter the Amalekites, had King David not put his faith in the protection of the King of Gath, then just maybe our families would remain safe at our side.

The murmurings in the camp are nearly palpable. Men often forget to remember God's protection as did King Saul which was discussed in earlier chapters. If David is blameless, if David is anointed and if David is upright, then why have these ills been visited upon our women and children? Mutiny springs from the depths of these grieved hearts.

Matthew Henry shares in his commentary on I Samuel 30, "Thus apt are we, when we are in trouble, to fly into a rage against those who are in any way the occasion of our trouble, while we overlook the divine providence, and have not that regard to the operations of God's hand in it which would silence our passions, and make us patient." (Henry)

These soldiers miss the divine providence of God's hand in what their eye's beheld. There are no dead bodies, so their loved ones could remain very much alive. Ziklag is still smoldering, so the Amalekites and their loved ones cannot be far away. But despair as fog can cloud a man's vision.

King David found himself in a tight spot. 1 Samuel 30.6 says, "And David was greatly distressed." (KJV) The word distress means "narrow". David had no room to maneuver. His army was openly talking of stoning him to death. David had nowhere to turn. David found himself between a rock and a hard place. His circumstances are dire. David has no way out.

Far too often God must resort to significant trials to regain the attention of a wayward man. After relying on his wits for months while living under the protection of the King of Gath,

King David is out of wiggle room. David is cornered and powerless.

King David in the distress of this situation, in the powerlessness of his own efforts returns to God for direction. In I Samuel 30:7-8 we read: "And David said to Abiathar the priest, Ahimelech's son, I pray thee, bring me hither the ephod. And Abiathar brought thither the ephod to David. And David enquired at the LORD, saying, Shall I pursue after this troop? shall I overtake them? And he answered him, Pursue: for thou shalt surely overtake them, and without fail recover all." (KJV)

The ephod is a garment which is thought to have been worn under the breastplate of the high priest or a Levite. The garment housed the Urim and Thummim. The Urim and Thummim are often considered to be precious stones, but their exact composition is unknown. This garment housing the Urim and Thummim is known as the oracle of Yahweh. Roman historian Josephus records that that the Urim and Thummim would emit rays of light in answer to questions where Yahweh's guidance and direction is sought.

God's answer recorded in this passage of I Samuel 30 shares the questions to which King David sought answers. The first question was, "Shall I pursue after this troop?" This question seems a bit odd given King David's long military training. King David knew the Amalekites could not have traveled a great distance with all the plunder, women and children that had been carried off. Ziklag is still burning when he and his army arrive, and the Amalekites have no reason to believe they would be pursued. The Amalekites perform prisoner interrogations, and those interrogations will reveal that the men of Ziklag are many days march away fighting with the Philistine King Achish. The Amalekites do not perceive any immediate threat, and the Amalekites will most certainly be surprised by a reprisal attack from the men of Ziklag.

Militarily there seems little reason for such an inquiry, so perhaps King David perceived the turn of events as a punishment visited upon he and his men for their actions over the preceding months. Perhaps King David wants to assure himself that these events are not punishments, and God is invested in what would be a battle where the wives, sons and daughters of his men will be in imminent danger. Perhaps King David envisions a trail of the dead bodies of wives, sons and daughters littering the ground as he pursues the Amalekites. David has his priest Abiathar and the ephod with him while he resides with Achish, King of Gath. King David now understands the great spiritual neglect he has exercised in not inquiring of the Lord concerning his seeking safety through a Philistine King Achish. King David asks God's permission to pursue and received an affirmative answer. Regardless of the motivation for the question King David returns to proper Godly order.

King David also asks divine guidance and understanding regarding the disposition of the wives and children. The Unim and Thummim responded, "and without fail recover all." Not one life will be lost in this rescue effort God tells King David.

With these divine answers from the oracle of Yahweh, King David is able to rally an army in despair. King David is able to convince this army that the path will not be littered with the bodies of their loved ones. King David shares with his men that God has promised all would be returned to them safely. So in pursuit of their families this six hundred man army marched.

All 600 members of his army willingly followed King David in pursuit of the Amalekites. King David might easily have estimate the size of the Amalekite contingent to be in the tens of thousands. David would need every one of his soldiers to confront such a large enemy force. But then his army reaches the Brook of Besor. Besor means cheerfulness. How difficult it is in the midst of tremendous trials that God presents an opportunity for cheerfulness. Besor was a stream filled with cold water running down from the surrounding hills. What a wonderful blessing provided by God to raise the esprit d'corp of an army that has spent the morning hours in pressed march under a hot sun.

The march from Ziklag to the Brook of Besor would not exceed fifteen miles. These men were marching on the coastal plain where the terrain would have not offered any great impediments to their forward progress. Today's military would expect a fully packed infantryman to cover 3 to 4 miles an hour under the conditions present south of Ziklag. King David's army travels to the Brook of Besor in three to four hours. After breaking camp these soldiers will have been at the Brook of Besor by noon.

For one in three this stop at "cheerfulness" is the spot where they quit. How many times does life confront individuals who spout out "What do you have to be happy and cheerful about?" amidst a trial. David's army has one-third of its contingent ask such a question. These folks turn aside and refuse to press on; they refuse to finish the race. The excuse is they were just too faint.

1 Samuel 30:10 shares, "But David pursued, he and four hundred men: for two hundred abode behind, which were so faint that they could not go over the Brook of Besor." (KJV) 200 out of 600 of King David's soldiers were so faint from the trials of the morning's fifteen mile march that they were devoid of faith in God's promises of the previous day. Were these men so physically fatigued and their physical strength so spent that they could not pass the Brook of Besor?

These two hundred stay behind and turn their backs on "and without fail recover all."

Certainly it wasn't the distance that generated the faintness of heart. That morning had been but a 15 mile stroll in the park for these battle hardened soldiers. The faintness was a product of what these soldiers witnessed on the trail. The Amalekite force was massive and the swath it cut through the country side was chilling. "And without fail recover all" had started to succumb to the overpowering weight of their empirical senses.

The issue at hand is not a question of the correctness of their military insight as much as a product of their empirical senses. Jumping ahead slightly to 1 Samuel 30:17 we find, "And David smote them from the twilight even unto the evening of the next day: and there escaped not a man of them, save four hundred young men, which rode upon camels, and fled." (KJV) For twenty-four hours King David and his 400 slaughtered Amalekites without losing one of their own. Let us speculate that each member of King David's force put to death *only one* Amalekite per hour. At this kill rate the Amalekites would have suffered 9600 deaths during the 24 hours of combat. If King David's army dispatched two Amalekite soldiers per hour during the battle the body count would have been 19,200 dead Amalekites. If each of David's men empowered and strengthened by God killed one Amalekite every fifteen minutes the death toll would have reached 38,400 dead Amalekites.

The 200 faint of heart men that remained at the Brook of Besor had rightly read the signs of the trail. How could this army of six hundred face a force that quite possibly outnumbered their force one thousand to one? The 200 men who stayed at the Brook of Besor make a flesh based and not a faith based decision. Even with God's help this group of soldiers has never been asked to face such long odds. These men could not bring themselves to believe "And without fail recover all".

What a dreadful curse these 200 men placed on their lives because of physical and spiritual fatigue. It is but a short time later the two hundred who stay behind witnessed the return of the 400 victorious soldiers who recover all. The initial moment of joy collapsed as the 200 view the faces of wives, sons and daughters. The penetrating stares burning into the 200 from their families spell out but one thought, "Really, you were too tired to fight for the lives of your family?" Or perhaps a wife said, "you had so little faith in God that you could not believe he would protect us?"

Would not these 200 faint of heart soldiers regret for the balance of their lives not having taken up arms that day against Amalekites. The depths of their souls cried out if I had only had enough faith in God to strengthen me during the day of the great battle, then I would not have had to endure the shame of my weakness in the moment of my family's greatest need.

The mighty men knew each other. The 400 would never forget the names of the 200. The 600 would never forget those who in exhausted anger called for the stoning of King David as Ziklag smoldered. There were no secrets and nowhere to hide weakness. The battlefield strips men of pretense. The bonds within this army are forged on the battlefield through a faith in God and King. These soldiers know who had their backs and who can be trusted.

Uriah the Hittite was a soldier who could be trusted. Uriah the Hittite was a friend in whom one could confide the deepest of secrets. Uriah was an honorable man and his exploits reveal it so. Uriah the Hittite was a comrade that would protect you with his life and in whom you would if necessary invest your life. The battlefield always tells the truth about the content of men's hearts.

Two verses from Timothy's writings in the New Testament bring the message home.

1Timothy 6:12 says, " Fight the good fight of faith, lay hold on eternal life, whereunto thou art also called, and hast professed a good profession before many witnesses." (KJV) The 200 at the Brook of Besor did not fight, they grasped too tightly to their physical well being, and they were left with no testimony to share in the day of great victory. So when challenged by a promise from God that seems impossible put on cheerfulness and wade into the fight, so at the end of the day you can say..........

2Timothy 4:7 "I have fought a good fight, I have finished my course, I have kept the faith." (KJV)

Chapter Sixteen

When does Uriah realize some respect? Location, location, location...

It is the story of the American dream becoming real for an American family. There are many organization and even television shows that feature down on their luck families being given homes of their own because the personal hardship and suffering or a life of service that forsook personal gain.

A blessing such as a new house is often realized only after many years of hard work. So it is with Uriah the Hittite. Uriah has been in loyal service to his King from the very beginning. Uriah is at King David's side since the Cave of Adullam. And now certain material blessings are flowing in the direction of Uriah the Hittite.

King Saul and nearly all of his family are dead. The political wars on who would ascend to King Saul's throne have finally subsided for there are many amongst the twelve tribes who did not recognize the anointing of David to be King by the prophet Samuel. Begrudgingly the twelve tribes of Israel slowly concede to the notion that David will be King over a united Israel, over all twelve tribes.

David is a member of the tribe of Judah. Following the death of King Saul David has successfully ruled over Judah for seven years. The last of King Saul's potential heirs to the throne have been murdered, and King David has their murders executed.

2 Samuel 5:1-3 shares what happened next, "Then came all the tribes of Israel to David unto Hebron, and spake, saying, Behold, we are thy bone and thy flesh. Also in time past, when Saul is king over us, thou ist he that leddest out and broughtest in Israel:

and the LORD said to thee, Thou shalt feed my people Israel, and thou shalt be a captain over Israel. So all the elders of Israel came to the king to Hebron; and king David made a league with them in Hebron before the LORD: and they anointed David king over Israel." (KJV)

So David is anointed by the leaders of the twelve tribes to be King over the nation. On occasion it often takes rebellious men years to line themselves up with God's purpose in their lives, but it is always right on God's timetable. God has anointed David to be King in his youth, and now as a man of 30 years the tribal leaders finally anoint David king. God's plan is being carried out in David's life and the life of the nation whether or not that realization always exists in David's mind and in the national consensus.

Upon assuming the reigns of the entire nation it is essential to establish a location from which to rule. There is in the middle of King David's newly united kingdom an enemy stronghold. Within the tribal territories of Benjamin existed a well fortified and walled city resting on a hill inhabited by Jebusites.

Jebusites are descendants of Canaanites who God intended for his people to eradicate from the Promised Land. Jebusites fall under the Canaanite curse to be "servants of servants" to the children of Israel. The responsibility falls upon the tribe of Benjamin to purge the land of this spiritual affront, but as with many of this tribe's other spiritual responsibilities the Benjaminites failed to follow through. So the responsibility is assumed by King David as his first task as the leader of the nation. King David will purge the nation of this spiritual Jebusite eyesore and return the ground to the possession of God. It is to be the new national capital, the City of David, Jerusalem.

Jerusalem is a city whose topography makes it difficult to attack. In ancient times occupation of the high ground is a significant advantage in war. Jerusalem has the high ground in abundance. But the industrious nature of the Canaanite inhabitants caused high walls to be added to the already menacing terrain which augments the Jebusite city's protection from attack. Little did the inhabitants know of the perspective from which King David and his army viewed this pile of stones. On top of city walls the Jebusites station the lame and blind of the city as lookouts and guards. The Jebusite military leadership thought so little of King David's army's abilities that the blind and lame men on the ramparts are ordered to hurl insults at King David's army. So great is the Jebusites' faith in a pile of rocks they call the city walls, nothing more is needed to protect the city. Blind men who could not see what developed and lame men who could not run for help are the guards for this arrogant godless people.

Dr. Donald Grey Barnhouse juxtaposed two events from his travels to Egypt in his profound work, The Invisible War. The passage is entitled The Laughter of God. King David's men viewed Jerusalem from the perspective of men strengthened by God to overcome a 100 to 1 man advantage during the recent battle with the Amalekites. A few high piles stones seemed like a small challenge to this army. Dr. Barnhouse's thoughts elucidate this army's perspective. Dr. Barnhouse says,

"The first time I came to the pyramids is by slow approach on the road and the slower gait of the camel. The weight of evidence of the ability of puny man is astounding, and one stood with no uncertain awe before these remnants of the seething energy of the ancient people. On a later occasion I came to the pyramids in the cabin of a stratoliner, flying up the coast of the Red Sea, enthralled with the tumbling ranges of mountains. We swung inland at dusk and the first lights of Cairo are beginning to twinkle. The earth is flat before us and from great altitude the pyramids could be discerned with difficulty. Then suddenly they could be clearly identified, tiny warts on the vast plain, excrescence upon the clean sandy desert. I entered into the laughter of God. It seemed to me that the sons of Ham, crawling like ants by the great river below, must have been the cause of the Holy Spirit's sad smile as He recorded the rage of the nations and the vain imagination of the people. " (Barnhouse)

Psalm 2:2-5 says, "The kings of the earth set themselves, and the rulers take counsel together against the Lord and against the anointed saying, Let us break their bands asunder, and cast away their cords from us. He that sitteth in the heavens shall laugh, the Lord shall have them in derision. Then shall he speak to them in his wrath and vex them in his sore displeasure" (KJV)

From the low and slow perspective of a man's view the pyramids of Egypt are awe inspiring, but from the reigning position of a God on high the pyramids are little more than sad laughable unwanted excrescence sitting in a pile of sand. King David and his army have a Godly perspective of the situation that day at Jerusalem. Every insult hurled by a blind Jebusite is answered by an Israelite sword. Every lame Jebusite hurling insults at King David probably learns to fly that day as they are thrown off the high walls to the waiting rocks below. When God speaks through his wrath and vexes men in His sore displeasure being on the receiving end of that displeasure is not a good spot to find oneself.

So the Jebusite city becomes that day the City of David. King David starts putting his stamp on his town immediately. Starting at the city walls a public works project is established rebuilding the city inward. But the Israelites are shepherd's and husbandmen and have sparse experience in the construction trades. So as always God willingly supplies their needs.

"The sons of the strangers shall build thy walls, and their kings shall minister unto thee," Isaiah would prophesy several hundred years later, but God's words are eternally true.

Once news of the consolidated kingdom and King David's rule being established in Jerusalem is spread abroad, King David starts to receive emissaries from surrounding nations. One of King David's first visitors is Hiram the King of Tyre. Tyre remains a city today and is located in southern Lebanon near Israel's northern border. Tyre is a wealthy Phoenician city and a busy port situated on the Mediterranean Sea, and Hiram is a King of great wealth.

Hiram offers and David accepts engineers and construction tradesmen to build David's palace and city. Hiram offers building materials the most valuable of which is the lumber from the Cedars of Lebanon. These cedars are massive trees 40-45 feet in circumference and upwards of 115 feet tall. The logistical efforts to transport such massive trees to Jerusalem are a huge expense, yet for David it is a free gift from God.

The property surrounding David's palace will also benefited from the expertise of the best beam and tenon tradesmen in the ancient word. Beautifully constructed private homes cascaded down the terraces leading from the opulence of King David's palace. The homes near the palace are an exclusive address not unlike the Hamptons or Beverly Hills. This is the best of the best neighborhoods, and King David hands out the keys to those homes. Uriah the Hittite, a mighty man, receives the home just below the King's balcony. Perhaps Uriah's home is in such close proximity to the King's balcony, so the King could immediately summons Uriah with a shout when David felt the need of protection or advice from one of his most experience military leaders. But since David designates who amongst his mighty men live where in his city, there is little doubt David knows exactly to whom the house and the roof beneath his windows belongs.

Uriah the Hittite's home has it all including location, location, location. What a wonderful place to lay his head after years of using his field pack for a pillow. The pauper in the Cave of Adullam is shedding his poverty. Uriah the Hittite is Movin' on Up to the eastside with a deluxe apartment in the sky.

Psalm 37:34 says, "Hope in the LORD and keep his way. He will exalt you to inherit the land; when the wicked are destroyed, you will see it." (KJV) Though the road be long and dangerous we are promised that if we sustain our hope and keep our faith, that the Lord's love will exalt us with an extraordinary inheritance. As for those sleepless nights visited by tossing and turning, when in our self pity we ask why the evil folks seem to be the ones getting all the blessings, well, sadly we will see those who embraced evil cut off and enter into an eternity of everlasting damnation.

Chapter Seventeen

Who are the players in the plot to kill Uriah the Hittite? "Every way of a man is right in his own eyes: but the LORD pondereth the hearts." Proverbs 21.2

The singularly remembered event in Uriah the Hittite's life story is King David and Bathsheba's adultery which leads to the subsequent murder of Uriah. But with murder there is always motive, and with motive there is an exercise of wills. God's will is being exercised by a man or women when operating within 2 Timothy 1.9. The New International Version of the Bible translates the verse "He has saved us and called us to a holy life—not because of anything we have done but because of his own purpose and grace. This grace is given us in Christ Jesus before the beginning of time..." (NIV) Satan many times through human history attempts to exercise his satanic will through the actions of men in opposition to God's will. And men and women when exercising their wills in a fashion inconsistent with the holy life to which they have been called, exercise their sinful Adamic nature which has been present in all men and women since the Fall.

Satan is the origin of sin in God's creation. Ezekiel 28:15 clearly states of Satan, "there is perfection in thy ways from the day thou ist created, till iniquity is found in thee." (KJV) Sin found its beginning in Lucifer whose name changes to Satan once he is ejected from heaven.

Satan is the fallen angel Lucifer. The angelic name Lucifer means 'light-bearer' and occurs just once in the entire Bible in Isaiah 14.12 according to Strong's Exhaustive Concordance. God entrusted Lucifer with the administration of all that God had created in the heavenly places prior to the beginning of time. It is through Lucifer that God communicated with his creation and through Lucifer all creation communicated with God. Lucifer administrated the responsibilities of government and priesthood. Lucifer is totally and completely bound and dependent on God for all that he directs. Lucifer carries God's light to God's creation and returned to God the worship and praise of creation.

The iniquity discovered in Lucifer is that of spiritual pride. Lucifer, when iniquity is discovered in him, has decided that he should be able to retain for himself a portion of the glory and honor he collects for delivery to the invisible Creator of all things. Lucifer is filled with a desire to claim for his own that which is not his to possess. Lucifer, a being created by God, decided that he is worthy to retain glory and honor that is due the Creator God. This selfish pride is the origin of sin. It is at that point Lucifer's name changes to Satan. Satan means adversary or enemy within the context of war. Satan now opposes God's will through calumny in an effort to erode obedience and destroy humility with an overweening sense of self. Give is simply replaced by take. Instead of giving glory, honor and power to Almighty God Satan attempts to keep that which belongs to God.

Then there are the billions of individual wills that belong to all living men and women that are exercised in man's sinful existence. In the Christian's Bible there is the creation story in the first book called Genesis. As the Genesis's creation story plays out we find the first man and the first women dwelling in a perfect existence and clothed by the righteousness of a life being lived under the will of the creator God. There is no need for a logical argument about ethical or moral behavior for there is no evil yet in existence which requires the prohibition of any human activities. The goodness, the morality, the truth of God's nature envelope the first couple in His omnipresence.

This perfect existence of the world's first couple carries with it but one small request of God. The couple is asked to exercise faith in their creator. Gen 2:16-17 shares, "And the LORD God commanded the man, saying, of every tree of the garden thou may freely eat: But of the tree of the knowledge of good and evil, thou shall not eat of it: for in the day that thou eat thereof thou shall surely die." (KJV) This couple can have faith in what God said and safely eat from any tree in their garden home save one. It would seem for quite some time the couple lived happily dining faithfully from the fruit trees God says are safe. They faithfully believe and remain compliant by not eating from the one prohibited tree that will kill them.

When I was young my mother would tell me not to touch the iron because it is hot, and it would burn my fingers. Well there was a day when I choose not to have faith in what my mother had told me. I touched the hot iron, and I burned my fingers. The couple in Genesis finally chooses to have faith in their decision making abilities to make an autonomous decision and exercise their own will, as I did with the hot iron. They choose not to have faith in what God said, and they too touched their hot iron. They eat from the one particular tree God said would kill them, and graveyards everywhere are filled with memorials to that one faithless action.

The master artist enters his studio. The artist owes no man and is not motivated by the receipt of a commission when exercising His infinite artistic abilities. He stretches His handmade canvas over a frame. Dyes and oils are mixed to create just the right color of paints required by the master for His masterpiece. The paints are applied to the palette. The master stands at His easel facing His canvas with palette and brush in hand creating a priceless masterpiece. Suddenly the brush rises up and says to the master artist, "I have no need of you to make sense out of this masterpiece. I have my own autonomous appreciation of this work of art. I am the final critic in the evaluation of this artwork." "Before we proceed," says the brush to the master, "you must agree that I don't need you to create this masterpiece. Because I know what is good from what is bad, and my soaring insight into this masterpiece is needed for the completion of this painting." And so the brush that is created by the master for the good pleasure of the master exercises its autonomous will desiring to make its mark on the masterpiece. In the exercise of that autonomy the brush falls from the faithful grip of the master's hand. The pompous brush falls into the muck the master treads under His feet. The brush forever misses the opportunity to participate in the completion of a masterpiece hanging in the universe's greatest museum throughout the ages. But then the master's hand reaches down to where the brush has fallen, reclaims the brush, and cleans the brush, and the brush hears the master say, "Brush you can do nothing out of my hand, but in my hand all things are possible." The brush responses, "Thank you Master for redeeming me from the muck and mire into which I had fallen, and I will remain faithfully in your hands."

For a Christian, faith is a substance and not an argument. Faith is the product of a relationship and not the end result of a logical conclusion. Through faith we choose to yield our autonomous will because we have learned through the exercise of that autonomous will we seem to repeatedly burn our fingers or fall onto the floor.

So what is the result of having a satanic will and man's will injected into God's Creation? One of the most heinous examples of the clash between God's will and man's will is the infamous question, "How could a loving God allow this to happen?" Millions of circumstances through the centuries have filled in the blank in this question. "How could a loving God allow that child to die?" "How could a loving God allow a mass murder such as Hitler to wipe out millions of lives in his ovens?" "How could a loving God allow terrible natural disasters?"

Well, if creation were left to the will of God men would still dwell in Eden without the presence of all the corruption that now befalls this world. When the will of Lucifer and the will of man first experienced by Adam in Eden entered creation God found it necessary to show all creation there is absolutely no hope in the exercise of any will apart from His. Creation must be shown that every exercise of Satanic will or human will is totally bankrupt.

In his work <u>The Invisible War</u> Dr. Donald Gray Barnhouse shares, "When we understand that God is continuing in patience with man until this lesson is fully set forth before the universe, we can understand the real purpose of history. Every thought and device conceivable to the mind of Satan and man must be explored and found wanting... One of the most visible differences between eternity and time is the difference between one will and more than one will... The quality of eternity is the fact that there is but one will - the will of God. The quality of time is that there is more than one will." (Barnhouse) There is no evil in eternity for evil exists only within time. When creation is again subject to only God's will then perfection will return.

Men need to accept that all that is destructive and evil in this world is a product of his own rebellion against God's will. God's verdict is that only the actions of His Son Jesus Christ provide man a path to return to a home under God's will. Jesus Christ's sacrifice is perfect and acceptable to His Father because Jesus always did what his Father told Him to do. Jesus Christ always exercised His Father's will and never His own will while walking this world incarnate.

So who are the players in this drama surrounding the murder of Uriah the Hittite? First there is Uriah the Hittite himself and the review of the will exercised by Uriah will be the last examined. King David and Bathsheba exercised their wills through this event. But there are other major willful influences that play a significant role in this sordid affair. Notable is Athithophel to which most casual observers of this story would respond "Who?" Athithophel is King David's most intimate and trusted advisor, and he is also Bathsheba's grandfather. There is Eliam who is along with Uriah the Hittite one of King David's mighty men and trusted warriors who has also been with King David since the Cave of Adullam. Eliam is also Bathsheba's father. The manipulative Bathsheba exercises her will in a variety of circumstances as the journey of her son Solomon being anointed King unfolds. And King David's rebellious son Absalom plays a significant role in revealing the will of Satan wound up in these events. With the examination of the motives behind the wills being exercised through these events a clearer picture of the extraordinary nature of Uriah the Hittite will unfold.

Chapter Eighteen

When does Uriah realize he is unequally yoked? When his trophy bride reveals her true colors...

As everyone familiar with these biblical events knows Uriah the Hittite is married to a women first introduced in the scriptures as Bathshua (1 Chron. 3:5) which translates to "daughter of wealth or opulence." (Strong) Bathshua's name changes between her scriptural introduction and her marriage to Uriah the Hittite. Prior to her marriage her name changes to Bathsheba which means "daughter of an oath."

So the "daughter of wealth" becomes the "daughter of an oath." Within the two names "daughter" remains constant, so it appears that her family changes her name at some point prior to her marriage to Uriah. Bathshua suggests that her family wants to make a statement regarding their personal social and financial status. Bathsheba's family is apparently of great wealth especially given the abilities of her grandfather Ahithophel which will be explored in coming pages.

An event or series of events occur that are of such significant in this young women's life that her family changes her name. Bathshua becomes Bathsheba, and the "daughter of an oath" now appears on the scene. Such a name changes begs the question what oath is taken that required a name change or why does "oath taking" needed reference in her name.

Matthew 5:33-35 shares Jesus Christ's view on oath taking, "Again, ye have heard that it hath been said by them of old time, Thou shalt not forswear thyself, but shalt perform unto the Lord thine oaths: But I say unto you, Swear not at all; neither by heaven; for it is God's throne: Nor by the earth; for it is his footstool: neither by Jerusalem; for it is the city of the great King." (KJV)

James 5:12 says, "But above all things, my brethren, swear not, neither by heaven, neither by the earth, neither by any other oath: but let your yea be yea; and your nay, nay; lest ye fall into condemnation." (KJV)

Jesus and then James through the power of the Holy Spirit encourages habitually truthfulness. When your yes means yes and your no means no there is no reason to take an oath. There is as the American Indian would say iron in the words of a truthful person. There is no need for an oath when unbendable words of iron are exchanged between truthful people.

Is the motivation for the name transition from Bathshua to Bathsheba an extraordinary event that required a personal oath be taken? Was Bathsheba's name to act as a constant reminder of that oath? Or is this young woman so habitually untruthful that her name is changed as a warning to those who have dealings with her? Or perhaps the name change relates to other circumstances, but the world seems to be filled with individuals so prone to prevarications each statement is followed with "I swear I am telling the truth." Nearly everyone has encountered the individual who has name dropped people they could have never met, or the individual who will interrupt a story about a spectacular personal achievement with their obviously untruthful one-upmanship, or the manipulator who will say anything to control a situation. Perhaps Bathshua is so pathological in her lying that a name change to Bathsheba is made necessary. If the later be true then Uriah the Hittite's trophy bride may have not revealed herself as the beautiful lying rich girl that her name changes may indicated. But within the family structure pathological or habitual lying is generally learned from and allowed by caregivers.

Psychologists today have learned that by the age of 4 years children understand how to mislead others through the use of prevarication. Often children do not receive the positive reinforce that develops a sense of self worth, so the child travels through life not feeling admired or popular amongst their peers or loved by their parents. Lying within these circumstances wrongly compensates children for their feelings of inadequacy and the lies do little more than reinforce the low self-esteem resulting from poor parenting. Children watch parents and learn manipulative behaviors as the child observes one parent attempt to control the other or as grandparents interject themselves in the lives of adult married offspring in an attempt to maintain control of the child as an adult. The evil parents who with threats of lost inheritance, with rejection or with abuse manipulate children are an example. Children develop into pathological liars as a result of neglect, lack of attention or unattainable goals. Another example might be a grade school student whose parents set extremely high performance standards and harshly condemn the child when the unrealistic goals are not achieved.

Bathsheba, given her family environment, may have developed into a pathological liar bent on achieving the highest status possible as a result of an abusive childhood. The Bible shares that Bathsheba is a beautiful woman and her actions recorded in scriptures indicate that she is an intelligent, involved and intuitive woman, but not a Godly woman as David's great grandmother the Moabitess Ruth. If Bathsheba's words to Uriah would have mirrored David's great grandmother's commitment to her mother-in-law Naomi in Ruth 1:16, "Entreat me not to leave thee, or to return from following after thee: for whither thou goest, I will go; and where thou lodgest, I will lodge: thy people shall be my people, and thy God my God: Where thou diest, will I die, and there will I be buried: the LORD do so to me, and more also, if ought but death part thee and me" (KJV) this story would have had a much different ending.

As with the name transition of Bathshua to Bathsheba so Bathsheba's father experiences a name transition in the Old Testament. Bathsheba's father is first introduced as Eliam. 2 Samuel 11:3 records, "And David sent and enquired after the woman. And one said, Is not this Bathsheba, the daughter of Eliam, the wife of Uriah the Hittite?" (KJV) Eliam translates as "God of the people" or "God is kinsman." 1Chronicles 3:5 speaks of the sons born to David by Bathsheba, "And these were born unto him in Jerusalem; Shimea, and Shobab, and Nathan, and Solomon, four, of Bathshua the daughter of Ammiel." (KJV) Ammiel translates" my kinsman is God" or "one of the family of God" or "servant or worshipper of God."

Eliam is one of David's mighty men. Eliam is the 28th mighty man mentioned as David identified these men in his last words. These men are with King David when he took refuge at the Cave of Adullam. These mighty men are counted in the four hundred who entered the Cave of Adullam in distress, in debt, and in discontent. Eliam joins himself with King David, and David became a captain over Eliam.

"My Kinsman is God" is an interesting combination of words. There is significant room to suggest that Eliam's father Ahithophel though Hebrew did not worship the God of the Hebrews. Ahithophel reached the summit of power, King David's most trusted advisor, but his advice is not God given or anointed.

So at this point in Eliam's life, at the Camp of Adullam, he may have found himself in such a state of anguish and distress that he is willing to join King David in an effort to escape the old and embrace a new life. Eliam may have borrowed heavily and found himself unable to repay his creditors. Eliam's father is most likely a man of great wealth which begs the question of why his father may have been unwilling to come to his aid at a time of major financial reverses. Eliam may have tired of his father's godless ways and emancipated himself from his father's household out of religious conviction.

Discontent can be better understood as bitterness. The motive for many at the Cave of Adullam is bitterness. Whether the bitterness is a product of political, family, financial or religious circumstance it is poison to the soul. Being drawn by God to a new life breaks the chain of bitterness that binds souls to the hurts of our lives rather than the freedom forgiveness provides. Our eyes are turned away from looking back at the chains that bind to looking forward to the freedom that the Life of Christ provides.

Chapter Nineteen

When does Uriah the Hittite understand the evil at play in high places? Ahithophel is Bathsheba's grandfather and King David's chief advisor, but Ahithophel has gone to the dance with the devil.

Athithophel is Bathsheba's grandfather. Ahithophel is the father of Bathsheba's father Eliam. Ahithophel is also King David's chief counselor which is established in 1 Chronicles 27:33, "And Ahithophel is the king's counselor." (KJV) Ahithophel's position in King David's leadership hierarchy is probably only second to the King David himself.

Yet a deeper look into Ahithophel's character reveals a sinister and diabolical character sold out to Satan with designs on the destruction of King David and King David's heirs. Ahithophel is Satan's man in this biblical drama working toward the destruction of God's redemptive plan for men established through His covenant with Abraham and His blessing on Abraham's descendants.

God establishes a plan through men to defeat Satan's rebellion. It is to be out of King David's line that Christ will come into this world. It is through King David's line that God has chosen to carry out the defeat of Satan's rebellion and the redemption of the universe. And Satan in all his twisted and perverse thinking is not about to leave God's efforts unchallenged. Satan is not a creative being, though Satan uses and reuses the converse of what God openly declares as righteous to entice men and women to fall away from God. Satan's attack of King David through Ahithophel is a subtle yet straight forward attack on the sinful proclivities of a King whose desires for God deteriorates under the onslaught of his pursuit of his fleshly sexual appetites and sinful nature.

Satan has not been dispossessed of the dominion God gives him over the earth. From his lightless imprisonment on a pitch black earth following iniquity being found in him to the moment God initiated the universe's redemptive process with, "Let there be light," Satan brooded for a fight. Satan's efforts remain unchanged from Eden. Enticing diplomatic words woo men and women away from their relationship with God through seductive temptations. Once seduced, Satan's goal is to gain the allegiance of the messed up man or woman.

Ahithophel is a man seduced by Satan's darkness, and a man who has pledged his allegiance to the enemy of God. As in the game of poker one must read the "tells" of the scriptures. One such tell of the nature and character of Ahithophel is found in 2 Samuel 16:23, "And the counsel of Ahithophel, which he counseled in those days, is as if a man had enquired at the oracle of God: so is all the counsel of Ahithophel both with David and with Absalom." (KJV)

Ahithophel's counsel is "as if a man enquired at the oracle of God." Athithophel is not a priest such as Samuel. Ahithophel did not consult the oracles of God, the Urim and Thummim, for the counsel he provides. Yet from the eyes of men the counsel provided by Ahithophel "is as if" it came from God himself. Ahithophel utilizes this satanic empowered ability to counsel men in an effort to build a platform from which he eventually will rule Israel, and his actions are straight from the satanic playbook.

So where or what did Ahithophel consult when producing advice for King David? Ahithophel's divinations and cleromancy according to rabbinical writings are a result of astrology. Satan is not an omnipotent or prophetic creature. But Satan does have one third of heaven's angelic hosts under his command for one third of heaven's angels are ejected with Lucifer when he is ejected from heaven. These beings have perfect memories and can move through the spiritual realm at the speed of thought. These fallen creatures are those numbered amongst the principalities, the powers, and the disembodied spirits known as demons. Satan has access to all real time data through this network, this cloud of demonic spiritual super computers. His spying network makes the NSA look like child's play because every relationship between every human being is stored in the memories of these demonic beings. Satan is an expert on exploiting the secrets of men and women. The counsel disbursed by Satan's agent Ahithophel through the false worship of the stars is based on the real time knowledge collected by Satan's host of minions.

Satan through Ahithophel's divinations could pass along valuable advice obtained through this demonic spy network. Ahithophel could relay real time information on enemy troop positions, he could advise as to the most advantageous time to attack an enemy, he could relay the whispers overheard in the dark corridors of power and he could provide counsel that played to the spiritual weaknesses of anyone seeking advice. The failure of Ahithophel's counsel is that it panders to the desires of Satan and the wills of men.

Were the Urim and Thummim consulted by King David then peace, order and righteous would have been the result. The counsel received from "the oracle of God" will speak the will of God. The counsel provided King David by Ahithophel deadened King David's ear to the voice of God and feeds King David's fleshly lusts.

It almost seems unbelievable that Ahithophel could have risen so high in King David's power hierarchy. The name Ahithophel translates "my brother is foolish", and the name has also been translated "the brother of the evil one." So what does the scripture say of a fool and one who embraces foolishness?

Proverbs 10:18 says, "He that hideth hatred with lying lips, and he that uttereth a slander, is a fool." Psalms 14:1 says, "The fool hath said in his heart, There is no God. They are corrupt, they have done abominable works, there is none that doeth good." Proverbs 14:16 says "A wise man feareth, and departeth from evil: but the fool rageth, and is confident." Proverbs 12:15 says, "The way of a fool is right in his own eyes: but he that hearkeneth unto counsel is wise." Proverbs 20:3 says, "It is an honour for a man to cease from strife: but every fool will be meddling." Proverbs 28:26 says, "He that trusteth in his own heart is a fool: but whoso walketh wisely, he shall be delivered." Proverbs 26:11 says, "As a dog returneth to his vomit, so a fool returneth to his folly." Proverbs 29:11 says, "A fool uttereth all his mind: but a wise man keepeth it in till afterwards." Proverbs 29:20 says, "Seest thou a man that is hasty in his words? there is more hope of a fool than of him." Ecclesiastes 4:5 says, "The fool foldeth his hands together, and eateth his own flesh." Ecclesiastes 10:12 says, "The words of a wise man's mouth are gracious; but the lips of a fool will swallow up himself." (KJV)

These verses all describe the actions of Ahithophel recorded in scripture. Ahithophel's counsel to King David regarding the affair with his granddaughter Bathsheba, to the subsequent cover-up, to his participation in Absalom's coup attempt and to his own suicide cries out of satanic influence. It is almost beyond comprehension that King David keeps close a counselor with fool in his name, but that is only half of the story. Ahithophel is from the town of Giloh. The name of this town translates "exile." So King David is being advised by "my brother is the evil one" from a town named "exile".

Ahithophel suffers from the same lack of humility as that of Satan and that weakness becomes his downfall. The magic like power exhibited by Ahithophel is most certainly a result of his satanic ties. He provides great assistance to King David on numerous occasions. Yet rabbinical literature records an event in which Ahithophel withheld advice from King David in the hope that he drowned in flooding that resulted from excavations for the construction of the Temple. The rabbinical literature indicates that through astrology Ahithophel is convinced that he would be King of Israel. So a man convinced by Satan through astrological worship that he would be King has the opportunity and motive to cut King David's life and reign short.

As a footnote Ahithophel's powers are well known through the ancient world and Midrashic rabbinical literature records that Socrates was a student of Ahithophel.

To view Ahithophel's evil actions through the knowledge of his satanic involvement plus his conviction that he would be King of Israel and deserved to be King of Israel, new intrigue emerges from this story. Let us conjecture that while lurking in the dark shadows Ahithophel advises King David not to join his army in the field knowing full well of King David's sexual appetites and roving eyes. Ahithophel would not be the first man whose lust for power allowed him to sacrifice, entice or enlist his granddaughter in an attempt to bring down a king. Little is beyond evil's darkness as is seen in the Middle East where parents sacrifice their children as suicide bombers.

It would have been impossible to contain the knowledge of King David's sexual adventures with Bathsheba within the walls of the palace. What would indicate Ahithophel would stoop so low as to engage his granddaughter in actions that would undermine the King? Ahithophel knows the Torah and is an expert at manipulating scriptural meaning. One need only remember Satan's manipulation in Matthew 4 of Christ after His forty days of fasting in the wilderness. If Ahithophel in his zeal for the throne assists in the creation either through commission or omission a violation of the law, then his counsel that could bring down King David. It would be very much in his character.

Ahithophel realigns himself with Absalom, David's son, during Absalom's coup attempt. Ahithophel in his lust for power recognizes that the Davidic line is coming apart at the seams, and he positioned himself to exploit the situation to his own benefit. Ahithophel efforts to destroy King David through the Bathsheba affair are thwarted by God. Now Ahithophel seizes the opportunity to position himself as Absalom's chief advisor and counselor.

Ahithophel offers advice to Absalom that will forever cement a divide between David and his son, and the same advice that would, were Absalom to become King, destroy his reign. Ahithophel advises Absalom to take the wives or concubines King David has left behind in his palace and have sex with all ten on the same roof King David observed Bathsheba bathing. The entire city would view the forbidden sexual abuse. Ahithophel's participation in giving this advice and his duplicity in the Bathsheba affair cries out Pro 26:11: "As a dog returneth to his vomit, so a fool returneth to his folly." (KJV)

Ahithophel in a final satanically motivated frenzy to kill King David offers up his final advice to Absalom. 2 Samuel 17:1-4 "Moreover Ahithophel said unto Absalom, Let me now choose out twelve thousand men, and I will arise and pursue after David this night: And I will come upon him while he is weary and weak handed, and will make him afraid: and all the people that are with him shall flee; and I will smite the king only: And I will bring back all the people unto thee: the man whom thou seekest is as if all returned: so all the people shall be in peace. And the saying pleased Absalom well, and all the elders of Israel." (KJV)

Ahithophel's satanic "I will" speech seems as music to the ears of a sexually intoxicated Absalom, yet inexplicably Absalom requests Hushai the Archite to provide his opinion. Hushai is an agent of King David attempting to thwart Ahithophel's advice to

Absalom. Absalom rejects Ahithophel's counsel and embraces Hushai's advice. It is a decision that will cost both Ahithophel and Absalom their lives.

It is again interesting to look at the meaning of the names of these individuals. The name Hushai translates to hasting. Hasting is the intransitive verb form of the noun haste. Hasting means rapidity of action, over eagerness to act and rash of headlong action. It is the nature of Ahithophel to deliver arrogant "I will" advice. Hushai, whose name is "haste" and who always charged headlong into action, speaks second. God's intervention in the speaking order revealed Ahithophel's satanic "I will" motivations and bloodlust for King David. Ahithophel's pride compels him to speak first and does not allow him to consider Absalom's desire for a second counselor, and so Proverbs 29:20 is to ring true for Ahithophel: "Seest thou a man that is hasty in his words? there is more hope of a fool than of him." (KJV)

So the foolish Ahithophel acts in haste. Ahithophel's advice encouraging Absalom to have intercourse with his father's wives places Absalom in an untenable position to be king. Deuteronomy 22:30 says, "A man shall not take his father's wife." (KJV) The law would not allow Absalom to remain king for long following King David's death. The abuse of King David's concubines is truly a heinous act and Ahithophel has positioned himself to put an end to Absalom following King David's death. Ahithophel's motives push for the immediate elimination of King David, but David remains Absalom's father. Absalom's desire to be king did not generate in him the same satanically motivated desire to murder King David that is found in Ahithophel's heart. Absalom is willing to delay the murder of his father. Ahithophel realizes the coup attempt would collapse without the immediate death of King David. So for Ahithophel all hope ends when Absalom delays action.

Ahithophel in his arrogant pride will not allow King David to seek him out and execute him for his crimes when the coup attempt ends. Ahithophel, as the unrepentant thief hanging with Jesus, will die shaking his fist at God. Ahithophel will snuff out God's great gift of life by his own hand. Ahithophel retreats to his hometown of "exile" and hangs himself.

Every Christian needs good counsel from time to time, but counsel needs to be sought from God, through the Word, and from godly men and women whose lives prove their faith.

Chapter Twenty

Is Uriah's marriage a forerunner of Hosea? Uriah marries the trophy bride knowing that compromised marriage vows will be a mirror into the heart of a King who has forsaken God.

Uriah the Hittite finds himself in the unique position to intimately know the heart of his King. Uriah has been with King David since the Cave of Adullam when everyone was in distress, and everyone was in debt, and everyone was discontent. Uriah gathers himself unto King David because he believes that David is truly anointed King of Israel. Uriah sees God's hand on this newly anointed King. Uriah unflinchingly extends to King David every honor and service due God's anointed.

As explored in earlier chapters Uriah the Hittite originally lives in or near the city of Gibeon. His Gibeonite ancestors gain their city's salvation from Joshua. As a people descended from Ham and Canaan they are ordered to live as "servants of servants" within God's proper order. The Gibeonites accepted that role and eventual became a group known as the Nethinims, the given or dedicated ones working in the Tabernacle. As a group "these servants of servants" are given to the Levites to serve as carriers of wood and water especially for worship in the Tabernacle.

The Uriah the Hittite is not of Hebrew decent. Gibeonites are a gentile people adopted into God's family. As a group the Gibeonites perform their temple duties flawlessly. Through their faithful delivery of wood and water to the Tabernacle for the "sin offerings" of the Jewish people, again they are renamed the Nethinims, the given ones.

For hundreds of years these "servants of servants" dedicate themselves to being completely sold out to God through their temple service. These Nethinims worked tirelessly to help a nation and a people wash away their sin. Day after day, week after week and year after year they witnessed the confession of every manner of wickedness known to man. The Nethinims knew the nature of sin, and they understood that the shedding of blood was the only path through which remission of that sin could be found and the stain of sin could be covered.

Uriah the Hittite watches his King increase his lands and wealth for over a decade while he also witnesses his King slip further and further from God's anointing. Uriah watches King David nurture his rebellious heart when his lack of trust in his God causes him to engage in battlefield acts meant to humiliate and bring fear to King Saul. First David cut King Saul's garment as King Saul slept in the cave David and his men were using as a hiding place. King David's uses a Jewish funeral tradition to send King Saul the message that he is a dead man walking. The demonstration is not directed by God.

On a second occasion King David clandestinely made his way into King Saul's' camp. Thankfully for David his faithful heavenly Father is there with His grace to protect him in his foolishness. God put everyone in the camp to sleep, so David wouldn't get himself killed. Yet once inside the camp standing next to the sleeping King Saul, David and his young nephew Abishai have a discussion about murdering King Saul. David said to his nephew Abishai, "The LORD forbid that I should stretch forth mine hand against the LORD'S anointed." It seems King David thought it prudent to continue to honor the Lord's desires by not ending the life of King Saul. Honoring God's commandment not to murder the anointed King Saul reveals that King David at this point in his life retained enough respect for God not to murder, but King David seems to turn his back on what he apparently believed were lesser of the Ten Commandments. King David steals King Saul's spear and water cup in absolute disregard of the eighth commandment of "Thou shalt not steal."

These faithless actions are meant to humiliate, dishonor and instill fear in King Saul. Worse these actions bolstered King David's sense of self-reliance. King David starts down a path without God. King David's vision becomes so clouded by his own fear and his ears so deafened to God's voice that he would not embrace God and the means God provides, the Urim and Thummim, to communicate with God. Instead King David establishes Ahithophel as his chief counselor. King David chooses a master in the dark art of astrology to give him advice on how to lead the nation. What an insult to the God who not only established his throne but created the nation on which the throne ruled! Ahithophel was the grandfather of the adulteress Bathsheba. Righteousness was not to be found in either Ahithophel or the easy Bathsheba, yet King David immerses himself in every manner of unrighteousness this family has to offer.

Who better to understand and recognize the deadness in King David's spirit than Uriah the Hittite? Uriah would have easily recognized the evil motivations of Ahithophel's self-serving advice to the King David. Uriah probably watched dumbfounded as King David utilized Ahithophel's counsel much like Christians today whose lives are brought to near ruin by the ear tickling words that promote men to do that which is right in their eyes. King David had provided no leadership to his children, and his children are left to rape and murder each other. David's heart is miles and years from the boy who in faith picked up the stones flung at the Philistine giant Goliath, and King David's trust in God has bleed away to the point he embraces the faux protection of a Philistine king.

Psalm 44:20-21 "If we have forgotten the name of our God, or stretched out our hands to a strange god; Shall not God search this out? for he knoweth the secrets of the heart." (KJV) It was no surprise to God that King David's heart is found in this sordid state, and it is no surprise that God would put in motion a plan to bring this prodigal son home.

God's plan of restoring a penitent heart in his anointed King reveals the infinite mercy bestowed on His elect. God treats no sin as little; but every sin is a forfeiture of the heavenly kingdom. It is only God's effort to make things anew in David's heart that prevents the momentum of David's headlong plunge into darkness from swallowing him.

The next to last of King David's wives and concubines is Bathsheba. The question is often asked was Bathsheba raped by King David as if this sexual immorality somehow exceeded the rabbinical indulgences allowing David eight wives and ten concubines. Can anyone seriously believe that King David sought out God's permission to engage in his predatory sexual nature when pursuing Bathsheba?

A more fundamental question to ponder is why did the faithful "servant of servants" Uriah the Hittite engage in a marriage with Bathsheba? Was it because of Bathsheba's beauty? Was it because Bathsheba was from a well placed rich and politically powerful family that could advance his career? Or was it because Uriah maintained his role as a servant and did what his God instructed him to do? There is nothing in the scriptural text that would indicate Uriah ever sacrificed his allegiance to his heavenly Father.

Instead God plans to deliver to King David through a prophetic statement via the mouth of Nathan the prophet a message regarding his adulterous affair with Bathsheba. The adulterous seeds King David has planted continue to grow in Israel. Many years later God spoke to the prophet Hosea and interpreted by Matthew Henry saying, "Now (saith God) Hosea, this people is to me such a dishonour, and such a grief and vexation, as a wife of whoredoms and children of whoredoms would be to thee. For the land has committed great whoredoms." (Henry)

The crack in the foundation of leadership will become a wide gulf in the heart and soul of those who follow. King Solomon was the son of King David who seceded to the throne. King David's drift into the sexual excess of eighteen women in his harem was exceeded greatly by King Solomon.

I Kings 11:1-6 shares, "But king Solomon loved many strange women, together with the daughter of Pharaoh, women of the Moabites, Ammonites, Edomites, Zidonians, and Hittites; Of the nations concerning which the LORD said unto the children of Israel, Ye shall not go in to them, neither shall they come in unto you: for surely they will turn away your heart after their gods: Solomon clave unto these in love. And he had seven hundred wives, princesses, and three hundred concubines: and his wives turned away his heart. For it came to pass, when Solomon was old, that his wives turned away his heart after other gods: and his heart was not perfect with the LORD his God, as was the heart of David his father. For Solomon went after Ashtoreth the goddess of the Zidonians, and after Milcom the abomination of the Ammonites. And Solomon did evil in the sight of the LORD, and went not fully after the LORD, as did David his father." (KJV)

King Solomon descends to the very depths of sexual sin. Seven hundred wives and three hundred concubines is not enough to satisfy King Solomon's cravings. King Solomon establishes in Israel the worship of sex and war through the principal female deity of the Phoenicians, Ashtoreth. Ashtoreth requires that the nation's young women sacrifice their chastity that is virginity in acts of temple worship. Sounds grand doesn't it? Bring all your daughters to the temple so every pedophile can worship through the rape of ten to fourteen year old young girls. But the untidy results of this temple worship are pregnant teenage girls. The unwanted babies born of rape are handled through the abominable practice of the Ammonites. The abortion mills of this age were not readily available to these teenagers, so these women carry their babies full term. Milcom, the abomination of the Ammonites, offers the nation a choice between the unwanted child and a nurtured child. In bringing an unwanted child to Milcom the ritual act of human sacrifice is practiced. Infanticide is King Solomon's choice to moral decay much like the "Choice" given the pregnant teenager who finds herself with child following a random sexual encounter.

So too did God have Uriah take Bathsheba as a wife that would be unfaithful in an effort to bring King David back to his senses. King David had been wallowing in his sexual sin for many years. The sensual pleasures of a soft bed and a women's touch cause him to rebel against his responsibilities to God and his kingship. God in his effort to purge his sons and daughters of their sinful proclivities will allow his children to embrace those proclivities, but God will not leave those who He has called to be His sons and daughters in that sin.

The New King James version translates Isaiah 57.16-19, "For I will not contend forever, Nor will I always be angry; For the spirit would fail before Me, And the souls which I have made. For the iniquity of his covetousness I was angry and struck him; I hid and was angry, And he went on backsliding in the way of his heart. I have seen his ways, and will heal him; I will also lead him, And restore comforts to him and to his mourners. I create the fruit of the lips: Peace, peace to him who is far off and to him who is near," says the LORD, "And I will heal him." (NKJV)

Like the prodigal son in Luke 15 David's backsliding has brought him to the point of demanding from God freedom from the responsibilities and restraints of the position into which God has anointed him. In 2 Samuel 11.1 we see, "And it came to pass, after the year was expired, at the time when kings go forth to battle, that David sent Joab, and his servants with him, and all Israel; and they destroyed the children of Ammon, and besieged Rabbah. But David tarried still at Jerusalem." (KJV)

To tarry means to sit yourself down. David sits himself down at home when it is time for him to be at work on the battlefield. He yields the responsibilities of his high office to his servants. God is on the battlefield, and David is in his Jerusalem palace enjoying the good life. King David is sleeping off the riotous living half way through the next day. 2 Samuel 11.2 shares, "And it came to pass in an evening tide, that David arose from off his bed." (KJV)

The great folly of King David is being content with less than God's best. King David is satisfied with the portion of his inheritance God has already placed in his hands. It is good enough for King David. David is weary of the weight that comes from God's governance of his life and living in God's house. David wants liberty from what he feels is God's heavy hand on his life. He wants the false liberty that is provided by sin. David is impatient of the confinement required by his high position and does not think himself master of his fate. Therefore King David chooses to break the bands of God that constrain his desires. He casts away the restraints of his Father's cords and instead embraces his own lust.

King David is in his palace. The Ark of the Covenant is on the battlefield. King David is outside the constraints levied by a leader. Hidden away from what he thought was his Father's view King David exercises a willingness to turn his back on the omniscience of God the Father. When the wicked don't believe their wickedness is observed by God for the sin that it is; then the depths of their embrace of that proclivity can be unlimited.

King David degenerates from ignoring his responsibilities to the laziness of sitting at home. Rather than engaging in his timely work he engages in riotous living. From riotous living King David's roving eyes bring him to adultery. In an effort to hide the folly of the unbridled restraint his adultery has caused, the wretched and miserable poor spirit found in King David only further aggravates the situation through an attempted cover-up. He refuses to return to his Father's house for forgiveness.

King David plunges ever deeper into the servile slavery of sin. As the prodigal son David seems satisfied with the solutions provided by his roll with the pigs. King David is to fill his belly with stealing another man's wife, murder, and tainting others with the fecal matter that rubs off him onto others. There is no relief from the state of sin King David finds himself but a return to his Father's house which he refuses.

King David has put himself under a sentence of death. The sinful state in which King David finds himself estranges him from everything that was good, virtuous and honorable found in his Father's house. The madness that possesses King David's heart and soul is astonishing. Proverbs 6:20-29 captures the nature of King David's fall.

"My son, keep thy father's commandment (King David didn't keep the commandments), and forsake not the law of thy mother: Bind them continually upon thine heart, and tie them about thy neck. When thou goest, it shall lead thee; when thou sleepest, it shall keep thee; and when thou awakest, it shall talk with thee. For the commandment is a lamp; and the law is light; and reproofs of instruction are the way of life: To keep thee from the evil woman, from the flattery of the tongue of a strange woman. Lust not after her beauty in thine heart; neither let her take thee with her eyelids. For by means of a whorish woman a man is brought to a piece of bread: and the adulteress will hunt for the precious life. Can a man take fire in his bosom, and his clothes not be burned? Can one go upon hot coals, and his feet not be burned? So he that goeth in to his neighbour's wife; whosoever toucheth her shall not be innocent." (KJV)

The end of King David's wild roving, the destruction of his foolish lusts, the softening of his hardened heart is as Isaiah described, "I have seen his ways, and will heal him; I will also lead him, and restore comforts to him and to his mourners." A sovereign God seeks out the wayward sheep and returns that sheep to His fold.

Sin always has its price. God recognizes the continuing slide of King David into his cesspool of sin. The message of penitence is to be delivered by the "servant of servants" Uriah the Hittite. Into whoredom Uriah was asked to marry. For King David this whorish woman, his neighbor Uriah's wife, costs Uriah the Hittite his life. It was not the taking of Uriah's life, but Uriah the Hittite giving his life that provides a path for the redemption for King David. Uriah's death opens the door to King David's repentance. Uriah the Hittite sacrifices himself to save his King which is what a "servant of servants" is trained to do.

Christian service does not come with the unalienable rights of life, liberty and a pursuit of happiness. Christians are called to relinquish all presumed rights in the service of the King of Kings and Lord of Lords. The Christian is a living sacrifice that through faith yields every right the flesh and this world claims. Christians are slaves to Christ who willing yield their freedom to Him. A Christian's pursuit of happiness can only be manifested through complete submission to the Master's pursuits. Christians are not their own. Christians are bought with a price and created for a purpose.

Rev 4:10 says, "The four and twenty elders fall down before him that sat on the throne, and worship him that liveth for ever and ever, and cast their crowns before the throne, saying, Thou art worthy, O Lord, to receive glory and honour and power: for thou hast created all things, and for thy pleasure they are and were created." (KJV)

When the Christian comes to the understanding that all glory, honor and praises is due the Lord, then they acknowledge Him by placing any reward or honor at His feet. Christians understand that their crowns are a product of His crown. Christians need to understand that their reward is their eternal ability to give glory to God.

Chapter Twenty-one

Is Uriah's wife Bathsheba raped by King David, or has the plan of a seductress capitalized on the voyeuristic predilections of a King with no sexual restraint and whose palace court knows his sexual weakness?

The drama and intrigue starts like a cheap paperback novel which only goes to show that the base unbridled nature of men and women when separated from God's influence always yields evil.

The biblical account is told in 2 Samuel 11:1-5,

"And it came to pass, after the year was expired, at the time when kings go forth to battle, that David sent Joab, and his servants with him, and all Israel; and they destroyed the children of Ammon, and besieged Rabbah. But David tarried still at Jerusalem. And it came to pass in an evening tide, that David arose from off his bed, and walked upon the roof of the king's house: and from the roof he saw a woman washing herself; and the woman was very beautiful to look upon. And David sent and enquired after the woman. And one said, Is not this Bathsheba, the daughter of Eliam, the wife of Uriah the Hittite? And David sent messengers, and took her; and she came in unto him, and he lay with her; for she was purified from her uncleanness: and she returned unto her house. And the woman conceived, and sent and told David, and said, I am with child." (KJV)

King David is in the wrong place at the wrong time. As discussed in the previous chapter King David's backsliding, like the prodigal son in Luke 15, has brought him to the point of demanding from God freedom from the responsibilities and restraints of the position into which God had anointed him. In the case of the prodigal son, the son left his father's house, and in

King David's case, God left King David in his palace and went to battle His army. King David stayed behind. King David tarried still at Jerusalem. King David sat on his inglorious butt while his men went about God's glorious work.

King David sits in the luxury of his palace consuming the best of wines and sumptuous meals while his soldiers are on the battlefield drinking out of nearest creek and eating C-ration type battlefield meals meant only for sustenance and survival. King David yields the responsibilities of his high office to his servants. God is on the battlefield and King David is in his Jerusalem palace enjoying the good life. King David is sleeping off the riotous night life half way through the next day. 2 Samuel 11.2 shares, "And it came to pass in an evening tide, that David arose from off his bed." (KJV) This time reference is for very late afternoon around the time the sun is setting. King David casts away the restraints of the battlefield and instead embraces his own lust.

At this point in King David's marital bliss he has accumulated 6 wives and 10 concubines. Wives and concubines were often part of the treaty making process in the ancient world, but for what type of man is 16 women not enough to service his sexual desires? King David has the ability to sleep with a different women each night and repeat the roster only twice per month. King David had what appears to be a compulsive need for sexual satisfaction. King David could easily be described in modern health terminology as a sex addict. Sex addicts are driven to seek out multiple partners and may perform sexual acts multiple times a day or night. King David's sex addiction interferes with his daily responsibilities. He certainly isn't going to the work God has set before him. David certainly doesn't seem to have the ability to stop his compulsive sexual behavior even when it means harm to his closest political adviser, to two of his mighty men, as well as to the woman involved. David uses his position as King as a means of dominance and control in the sexual liaisons. David uses his political power and soldiers to escort Bathsheba into his presence and creates the compromising situation. King David knows the negative impact such activity could have on his kingship and life were his secrets to be revealed, yet he enters into the activity without regard to the consequences. And King David clearly feels no remorse for his actions which is not unlike a recent American president who looked into cameras and lied to a nation about activities with a student intern in room off the White House's Oval Office. King David is out of control, and everyone seems to know it but him.

Let us move to where King David is and what he knows about where he is. David arose from off his bed, and walks upon the roof of the his house: King David is on the roof of his new house. David's house is surrounded by all the other new houses he has had built through the graciousness of God's supply through Hiram the King of Tyre. In Chapter 16 it was discussed that King David wasted little time putting his stamp on his town. Starting at the city walls a public works project is established rebuilding the city inward. All issues regarding God's law and public sanitation were incorporated into the city's rebuilding. The City of David's waterworks are some of the most advanced in the ancient world.

But the Israelites are farmers and tent dwelling husbandmen, and as a general population have sparse experience in the construction trades. Hiram the King of Tyre volunteers as project manager and supplies all the city building know how as well as the vast majority of building supplies.

Tyre remains a city today and is located in southern Lebanon present day Israel's northern neighboring nation. Tyre is a wealthy Phoenician city and busy port situated on the Mediterranean Sea and so also is Tyre's King Hiram of great wealth. Hiram's engineers and construction tradesmen build David's palace and city. Hiram offers building materials the most valuable of which is the lumber from the Cedars of Lebanon. It was the best of the best neighborhoods, and King David hands out the keys to those homes. Money can't buy these homes.

Uriah the Hittite, a mighty man, received the home just below the King's balcony as we discover given the location of his roof. Perhaps Uriah's home was in such close proximity to the King's balcony, so the King could immediately summons Uriah with a shout when David felt the need of protection or advice from one of his most experience military leaders. Since David would have designated who amongst his mighty men lived where in his city, there is little doubt David knew exactly to whom the house beneath his windows belonged.

King David has undoubtedly looked out across the blessing God has bestowed on the City of David. He has watched those who he has been able to bless enjoy their new homes. After years of sleeping next to his mighty men in caves or on the hard ground around a thousand campsites, David knows their pleasure. One only needs to ask, "If I were able to give a close friend a house, would I in just a short time forget the location of the house with which I blessed the friend?"

So David walks around on the roof of his palace. King David's palace is built on one of the highest points in the City of David. King David's house occupies the high ground, and there was no house above his house. King David's roof top provides a spectacular view of the city, the Kidron Valley across to the Mount of Olives and the Central Valley. Nothing impedes his view for miles in any direction save Mount Moriah.

From this vantage point and after waking from a night of riotous living King David's roving eyes brought him to adultery. Were a high power telescope available to King David he would have readily employed its magnifying powers as do coin powered telescope satisfy a tourist to enjoy scenic views from the spectacular advantage of great height. Wiping the hang-over from his voyeuristic eyes, his gaze falls upon a naked woman bathing on Uriah the Hittite's roof. As the biblical text states, "he saw a woman washing herself; and the woman was very beautiful to look upon."

The first seven times the word "saw" appears in the Bible are in the first chapter of its first book of Genesis. Here the phrase "God saw that it was good" repeats throughout that first chapter. God looked at all the wonderful things that he had made and recognizes his creation as good. It was pleasant and agreeable to look at and pleasing to all the senses.

The manner in which King David rests his eyes on the bathing Bathsheba is not the same look God had when He looks upon his creation. King David's look is that of a fallen man and has its roots in Genesis 3:6. The verse shares, "And when the woman saw that the tree was good for food, and that it was pleasant to the eyes, and a tree to be desired to make one wise, she took of the fruit thereof, and did eat, and gave also unto her husband with her; and he did eat." (KJV) Here too Eve was walking in a place that brought her into the position to be deceived. Lust is conceived in her heart for the fruit God told her not to partake. She brings the fruit of which she has partaken to her husband, and Adam chooses to eat thereof. Lust is conceived in King David's heart, he has the fruit brought to him, and of that fruit he does partake. As Hebrews 11.25 shares sin can be pleasurable for a season. Was it one month or perhaps two without a menstrual cycle before Bathsheba knew she was with child and contacted King David? The sin was pleasurable for a season.

When the wicked don't believe their wickedness is observed by God for the sin that it is then the depths of their embrace of that proclivity can be unlimited. King David initiates an attempted cover-up as he continues to plunge ever deeper into the servile slavery of sin.

King David is a man out of control. For those living within hearing distance of the palace porches his habits would have been no surprise. For how many days since his soldiers went to the battlefield has King David been on the prowl from his roof top perch? If King David can see everyone from his roof top vantage point, then everyone who cares to look up can see him. So this knowledge that the King is walking the roof top in late afternoon should preclude any activities that the neighbors did not want their King to see. The potential of being observed is great because King David will have guards and lookouts stationed to protect a city whose army is away from the city at war. Not protecting the family and children of his men is a lesson sorely learned at Ziklag of which this book has previously discussed.

So from the roof King David sees a woman washing herself; and the woman was very beautiful to look upon. It cannot be assumed with deference to the number of eyes looking down from this military and personal vantage point of the King's roof that Bathsheba is embracing modesty in her public display of nakedness.

We are told in the scriptural reference that Bathsheba was bathing, 'for she had purified herself from her uncleanness.' The ritual bath or mikveh is a Jewish tradition traced to the requirements for cleanliness recorded in the Levitical law. Kosher Jewish women are required by Levitical law to immerse themselves following their menstruation and childbirth to again become ritually pure and are then permitted to resume an intimate relationship with their spouse. A truly kosher mikveh requires the bather to be immersed in "living water" in a ritual act of purification. The water must be stationary rain water, spring water, lake water, ocean water or river water. During the mikveh men and women are to immerse themselves and say prayers in a recognition of the transition that is taking place in their life.

Though a roof is a likely place to collect rain water it seems a unlikely place to contain a large bath. The roof would need to sustain the weight of a water filled cistern, a bathing pool large enough for immersion and the bather as well as a means to discard the soiled water. The mikveh is usually a common bath that services a community where the pools are serviced by those trained in maintaining the baths as kosher. The pools are general hewn out of stone. The filling and draining of these ritual baths would have been incorporated into the building plans of The City of David executed by King Hiram and his urban planners. Though Bathsheba may have been bathing on her roof top, it seems highly unlikely that she was executing the mikveh in a fashion consistent with immersion ritual.

From Bathsheba's roof-top display King David can conclude three things. First, Bathsheba is a beautiful woman which sends King David's sexual addiction into overdrive. Second, because she is bathing on her roof-top for any and all to see and not in the mikveh King David could conclude that Bathsheba was not a highly spiritual young woman. Thirdly King David realizes that Bathsheba was at that point of her menstrual cycle where she would be most receptive to sexual activity. Some will argue that King David is concerned about Bathsheba's ritual cleanliness in an effort to argue that David had true fillings of love for Bathsheba. It is important to note in the text that Bathsheba's ritual cleanliness is not mentioned until after her intercourse with King David. King David's actions are those of a sexual predator seeking self gratification through the power and position God has anointed him. Bathsheba willingly, as Eve did, brings the fruit to King David for his consumption. There is no scriptural evidence that either party resists entering into this sexual union, though both are quite aware of the commandment against adultery.

Following the intercourse if either party was truly interested in ritual cleanliness, both are required to act. Lev 15:15-17 says, "And the priest shall offer them, the one for a sin offering, and the other for a burnt offering; and the priest shall make an atonement for him before the LORD for his issue. And if any man's seed of copulation go out from him, then he shall wash all his flesh in water, and be unclean until the evening. And every garment, and every skin, whereon is the seed of copulation, shall be washed with water, and be unclean until the evening." (KJV)

There is no scriptural record of either party in this sordid affair being spiritual enough to bath as required by the law following the copulation. Could it be that both parties know the heinous nature of their act and prefer to keep the act secret? Could the sexual predator willing to commit adultery not give a second thought to ritual cleanliness? Would the temptress know her plan to sexually seduce the King would be revealed by the need for a second mikveh in less than a day?

But let us return to actions prior to the act of adultery. In II Samuel 11.3 we find King David engaged in essentially two commands, "And David sent and enquired after the woman. And one said, Is not this Bathsheba, the daughter of Eliam, the wife of Uriah the Hittite?" (KJV)

So King David first sends for the woman to be brought to him. Second King David is said to enquire after the women. With a Strong's Concordance it can easily be determined that this translation can be a bit confusing. The word translated in II Samuel 11.3 as "enquired" is more than twice as many times translated as "seek" in the Old Testament. The Old Testament phrase most often linked to this word is "seek the Lord". King David has told his servants not only who he wants them to bring to him but the King provides them direction on the emphasis and enthusiasm with which they are charged to collect this woman. The servants are to seek out this women as if they were seeking the Lord. David is seeking out sin with the same passion he should be seeking the Lord!

The King commands his servants to go get this woman and don't come back without her. Was the emphatic nature of King David's command because he knew he might receive the protest that he in fact did receive from his servants? The servants clearly understood the sexually deviate nature incorporated in King David's request. The ensuing protest was, "Is not this Bathsheba, the daughter of Eliam, the wife of Uriah the Hittite?" King David knew that this was the wife of his highly regarded friend and mighty man Uriah the Hittite. The servants all knew that the women they had been ordered to fetch was the wife of their friend Uriah the Hittite. Yet the sex drunk King David brushes aside his servant's protest not to drink and drive, and the King demands the car keys to be brought to him.

Due to the confusing nature of the translation of II Samuel 11.3 many are left with the understanding that King David did not know who the hot chick was bathing on his neighbor Uriah the Hittite's roof. Of course King David knew this woman was Uriah the Hittite's wife. This family was one of thirty families who lived together in tents and dined together a thousand times around campfires for over ten years.

King David would have most assuredly attended Uriah and Bathsheba's wedding. Would King David have insulted his chief and closest adviser Ahithophel who was Bathsheba's grandfather by failing to attend the Uriah and Bathsheba wedding? Would King David have insulted two of his mighty men, Knight's at his King Arthur's round table, by not attending? No investigative reporter worth his salt would make the obtuse conclusion that David didn't know this woman. Rather the good reporter concludes Bathsheba's beauty has burned into this sexual predator's psyche. The opportunity has presented itself or rather the King may have created the opportunity to satisfy his lust for Bathsheba. King David knows that Uriah the Hittite is miles away on the battlefield. King David acts upon a fantasy that he has relived in his mind with the sighting of Bathsheba. King David makes his move come hell or high water.

Is there recorded in scripture of one whimper from the willing Bathsheba? Does Bathsheba resists to the point of the righteous Queen Esther and utter those spirit filled words, "If I perish, I perish" found in Ester 4.17. (KJV) Were Bathsheba to have uttered these faith-filled words that David's great great grandmother Ruth uttered in Ruth 1:16-17 in defense of her husband, "And Ruth said, Intreat me not to leave thee, or to return from following after thee: for whither thou goest, I will go; and where thou lodgest, I will lodge: thy people shall be my people, and thy God my God: Where thou diest, will I die, and there will I be buried: the LORD do so to me, and more also, if ought but death part thee and me;" (KJV) then perhaps King David would have turned away in shame.

So the desires of two willing partners, in an expression known in modern vernacular as an open marriage, take a roll in the sack. No harm no foul they say. Who will ever know? It is just harmless sexual pleasure between two consenting adults. Yet Uriah the Hittite will die as a result of this poisonous embrace.

In a country like the United States where people by the millions view sexual intimacy as a sporting event, God's teaching on adultery and fornication is disregarded. Hearts are hardened to the destructiveness of sexual relationships outside the fidelity of marriage. Wedding covenants made to God are easily cast aside by society. Men and women must guard their hearts and minds for Christ has revealed that if you have done the act in your head, it is the same as doing the act in a bed.

Chapter Twenty-two

Is the scandalous affair between David and Bathsheba to become a spectacle flaunted in the face of a city and the army, or do the participating parties retreat in shame and attempt to cover the sin?

The City of David is a military town. The city's massive stone walls provide a safe harbor for residents were an attack to come. King David has conquered the city and turned the city into the new national capital and seat of power for all Israel. The city is filled with his advisers, military leaders and their families. The city's high walls protected those who the soldiers leave behind when off to the battlefield they march. The families already tightly bound together through over a decade of campfire living provide each other moral and physical support. No the city didn't have today's social media to propagate gossip while they kept themselves locked down in their homes, but news still travels quickly with each neighbor having real time face time over the back fence.

All the important issues of the day pass up and down the road up the mountain as messengers and soldiers travel to and from King David's version of the American White House. Streets fill with people who would observe all that pass by with particular note being taken of those who enter and depart the King's palace. Had the paparazzi with their cameras been alive and well at this time pictures of all who enter and depart the palace would be seen in every grocery store tabloid. To assume the appetite for gossip is any less voracious in the day of King David as in the day of Princess Diana can only be the product of an addle mind. Of course the gossip mongers collect around the gates of the palace to observe and spread all that transpires. A possibility exists that there were those who paid these prying eyes for every juicy morsel of untoward knowledge.

Given human nature it seems impossible word would not have quickly spread throughout the city of all who enter and depart the palace. The gossip mongers will record when a guest entered and when the guest departed. All the tidbits would be for sale to the King's enemies.

The nation is at war with their ancient enemy Ammon. Israel has besieged the Ammonite capital city of Rabbah on the east side of the Jordan River while King David enjoys his evening of illicit delight. It is worth noting the nature of this Ammonite enemy of God. These are Canaanite people, who have not been destroyed when the nation entered the Promised Land, but from whom did the Ammonites descended and why were the Ammonites so despised by God?

For the story of Ammon we must visit Genesis chapter's 15, 18 and 19. The first thing to take note in Genesis 18 is the visit of Christ and two angels to the tent of Abraham. The angelic visit is to inform Abraham and Sarah that God is about to fulfill his promise made in Genesis 15 to give the couple a child.

God has promised Abraham and Sarah decedents, yet Abraham and his wife Sarah have no children. At the time of the angelic visit in Genesis chapter 18 Sarah has already been through menopause. Sarah is no longer able to bear a child without the miraculous intervention of God. Sarah's hope of a child from her womb died with the drying up of her womb. She isn't able to bear children, and she knows it.

After years of waiting for the conception of a heir Sarah's embittered soul concocts a plan to provide her husband a son. It will not be a son of God's own choosing, but a son of Sarah's faithlessness. Sarah's plan dismisses God's plan of using the womb of the wife with whom God blessed Abraham. Sarah's plan is to use the womb of another woman to provide a man made version of God's plan.

Sarah's lack of faith in the promise made by God to this couple years before causes her to attempt to force God's hand. Sarah as Eve brought to her husband an apple to eat. Abraham like Adam did at his wife behest eat to the apple of Sarah's maid servant Hagar. Hagar conceived and bore the spurious offspring Ishmael to Abraham. Ishmael is the son of the faithless act of Sarah in seeking a family for her husband without God's blessing. Sarah, Hagar and Abraham's man-made solution to God's promise for a son for Abraham and Sarah is, and please forgive the double entendre, an act of the flesh.

So in the heat of the day the Lord and two angels arrive at Abraham's camp. Abraham is sitting in his tent enjoying the shade when he looks up and sees the Lord and two angels standing at the opening to his tent. Abraham immediately recognizes the Lord and his angelic companions, runs to them and bows down to them.

Abraham desires to honor, respect and care for every need these visitors might have explodes through his tremendous hospitality. Abraham provides water to wash the visitors' feet. Abraham asked Sarah to cook cakes for these visitors. Abraham ran to his herders and told them to select and butcher a tender and good calf for a meal of meat for the visitors. The visitors eat and drink of the all that is brought to them by Abraham.

After the meal is finished, the Lord asks a question of Abraham which at first blush seems relatively simple. The Lord asks, "Where is Sarah thy wife?" It is worthy of note that the Lord did not ask "Where are Sarah and Hagar your wives?" or "Where is your son Ishmael?" There is no recognition by the Lord of Hagar or Ishmael in unfolding of these events.

Abraham answers the Lord's query with the response, "Behold, in the tent." God is omniscient and omnipresent. God knows Sarah is listening while hidden from view behind the tent's opening. God is just saying Sarah, if you want to hear something good, listen to what I am about to share.

With her ear stuck to the side of the tent, Sarah hears the Lord tell Abraham, "Abraham, I will return in nine months and your wife Sarah will have the baby I promised you." At this point Abraham is 100 years old and Sarah is 90 years old. At times, Sarah doubted God, and this is one of those times.

The Irish say a burden too long carried makes a stone of the heart. Sarah has waited so long for a child to fill her empty arms that she now has given up on hope. When she heard what God said about having a baby at 90 years old a sarcastic "Yah sure," bubbled up in her heart. The expression of doubt is heard all the way to heaven even though not a sound is made. It is one of those moments when someone dangerously darts a car through traffic nearly causing you to wreak, and at that moment something profane percolates up out of your soul and out of your mouth rather than praise to God for maintaining your safety.

The Lord heard what was in Sarah's heart. He calls her out, and Sarah lies in an attempted cover-up what is in her heart. Telling a lie to God, what is she thinking? Nobody is buying the lie. Later the centenarian Abraham and the nonagenarian Sarah embraced in faith God's promise and reproductive life is miraculously restored to their bodies and an infant son is born.

God sees through the faithless confessions of our hearts. King David should have realized that the confession, "I did not have sex with that women" is not the type of confession God demands.

The two angelic visitors to Abraham's camp depart for the twin cities of Sodom and Gomorrah. God said to Abraham, "Because the cry of Sodom and Gomorrah is great, and because their sin is very grievous" the cities would be destroyed." Abraham's intercessory prayers could not identify 10 righteous men in these cities. The only people who would be saved from the destruction of these two cities are Abraham's nephew Lot, Lot's wife who is a child of Sodom and Lot's two daughters who has been reared in Sodom.

Waiting at Sodom's gate is Abraham's nephew Lot. Lot immediately recognizes these visitors as angelic beings and rather than subject them to the horrors of a night in the streets of Sodom, Lot press the two angels to stay in his house that even. The angels relent to the press of Lot's repeated requests and stay in his house. But the stay in Lot's home did not stop what is to unfold in the streets as the city's men demand new human male flesh for sexual consumption. The presence of the angels turned the Sodomites into fiendish lust driven creatures.

Years later the same story plays out with the tribe of Benjamin. As readers may recall the Levite priest's wife is offered to the murderous sexual appetites of the residents of Gibeah when the men of the town all demand the Levite priest for the satisfaction of their sexual frenzy. The Levite's wife is thrown to the crowd and dies from the repeated sexual assaults.

Lot offers his two daughters to the crowd outside his door. This offer of female flesh is disregard by the crowd of Sodomite men. The crowd continues their demand for the angelic flesh. To beat back the attack on Lot's dwelling the angels strike every man in the Sodomite crowd with blindness. The husbands of both Lot's daughters are in the crowd outside Lot's home, but apparently not among those struck blind. Yet even as blind men their devilish sexual cravings continue to drive them to find the door of Lot's home. It is a bad scene out of a zombie movie.

The angels reveal God's plan to destroy the cities of Sodom and Gomorrah, and inform Lot that he must gather his family and depart the city. Lot and his family cannot look back. It is the same message, "don't look back" that is discussed in previous chapters regarding King Saul.

Lot's sons-in-law decline the opportunity for safety and refuse to leave with their wives. Lot argues with the angels about the destruction of Zoar, and begs the angels that that city named "Insignificant" might be his family's refuge. Zoar is given a brief reprieve but will eventual be consumed by the rising waters of what will be the Dead Sea.

Lot's wife looks back at the destruction of Sodom and Gomorrah and dies in the disobedient act much like the beloved Rachael. Lot's daughters realize their husbands cannot survive the destruction. Lot fears staying in Zoar and retreats to a cave in the mountains for the safety

Lot may have thought himself free from the sexual attacks constantly present in Sodom and Gomorrah. He is alone with his daughters hidden away in caves for protection from all manner of evil. But the evil found in isolation is usually an evil from within.

Lot's daughters' husbands are killed by the fire and brimstone that rains down on the cities. Hidden away in mountain caves surround by Canaanites the sisters are left with no worldly hope of new husbands and families. So the sisters hatch a plan born of the same sexual perversion out of which they were just delivered. The sister's future will not be in the hands of the God of Abraham, but their future will be one of their own creation. Sons are needed to provide care when Lot dies of old age and the future of the family name needs to continue.

So a wicked plot is conceived out of the ashes of Sodom and Gomorrah by Lot's daughters. The daughter's will make their father drunk with wine. In his diminished condition the daughters will have sexual intercourse with their own father in the hope of becoming pregnant and thus provide for themselves a future. The event harkens back to those of Noah's tent.

Matthew Henry in his commentary of Genesis 19 states, "The sight of God's most tremendous judgments upon sinners will not of itself, without the grace of God, restrain evil hearts from evil practices: one would wonder how the fire of lust could possibly kindle upon those, who have so lately been the eye-witnesses of Sodom's flames." (Henry)

The actions of Lot's daughters produce two sons and heirs both hated by God. The names of these two sons produced in incest were Moab and Ammon. While Israel is on the battlefield attempting to eradicate the plague that erupted out of the ash hemp of Sodom and Gomorrah, while Uriah the Hittite is on the field of battle destroying Ammon, King David remains in his palace practicing the same sexual perversions his God is attempting to destroy across the Jordan River. The situation is quite the curious juxtaposition oblivious to a King who is wallowing in a sexual cesspool. Like the blinded men of Sodom crawling over each other looking for Lot's door, King David didn't care who saw his sexual sin. All eyes that could see were on King David, and those eyes could see the filth in which he is living.

In the City of David every eye diligently sought out the battlefield messengers. When the King sent his messengers to retrieve Bathsheba the only thought amongst all who observe in this military town is something has happened to Uriah the Hittite. But Bathsheba is gone for a long time.

Eyes remain peeled for Bathsheba's return from the palace. How long does it take to inform a wife of the death of her husband? How much consolation can a King provide? Minutes stretch to hours and Bathsheba still does not return home. Neighbors and servants anxiously await the news, but no news comes. Then in the early morning Bathsheba returns quietly to her home. There is no news of the death of her husband. Uriah remains faithfully at his post on the battlefield. Inquiring minds ask, "If Bathsheba's visit to the palace is not to inform her of the death of her husband and provide hours of consolation, then why did she remain in the King's palace all night?

Some unnamed source within King David's palace who feels the righteous indignation of the King's actions shares the inside scoop. King David took Uriah the Hittite's wife to bed. The two of them committed adultery in the King's bedroom. Is it one of the King's guard or messengers, is it one of the King's wives or is it a one of the King's ten concubine that started the rumor mill rolling? Many saw what transpired, and many share what they witnessed. From mouth to mouth the story spreads like wildfire. The King had sex with Uriah the Hittite's wife Bathsheba.

As supplies are carried to sustain men on the battlefield, so are the stories from home. The King is not in his place leading the army, and now rumors carried by servants and family share with the soldiers their King has taken to bed the wife of an immensely respected soldier. The King committed adultery with one of his mighty men's spouse. How could it be?

Uriah the Hittite will hear the buzz of rumors. Uriah may very well have been told directly by a friend of the situation back home. It certainly wouldn't be the first time a lonely soldier's wife strays to another man's bed. It certainly won't be the last time a person in great power would speak to his people, his friend, his wife, and to the parent's of the offended women and say, "I did not have sex with that women."

After several months the call comes for Uriah the Hittite to return to the City of David. Perhaps one of Uriah's faithful servants shares with him during the delivery of supplies that his wife has missed a couple of her periods and is very distraught.

What is Uriah the Hittite to do when he faces King David? Uriah has had a considerable amount of time to consider this question. The time of facing King David and his wife Bathsheba is to be soon at hand. What is a "servant of servants" to do? Greater love has no man than he who gives up his life for a friend.

Chapter Twenty-three

With the knowledge of his wife cheating with his lust driven King what is Uriah the Hittite to do when he comes face to face with the wretched man who impregnated his wife and abused his trust?

The overheard rumors and conversations with close confidantes buzz through Uriah the Hittite's mind. Uriah has had days if not weeks to consider what events may reside in his future and what his response to this situation might be. Bathsheba is pregnant with a child not of his loins. The law makes it clear what can be done with Bathsheba and King David. King David must make a move, but what will it be? Uriah will have to respond when the confrontation arrives, yet how should he respond?

The sordid talk of the palace intrigue circulates for weeks. Those servants in Uriah's house have learned how to faithfully serve from a master who taught them by action and not by word. The servants carry word to Uriah of the pregnancy of his wife. Infidelity is now compounded by living proof growing in his cherished Bathsheba's womb.

The story unfolds in 2 Samuel 11:5-6, "And the woman conceived, and sent and told David, and said, I am with child. And David sent to Joab, saying, Send me Uriah the Hittite. And Joab sent Uriah to David." (KJV)

Was this plan premeditated by King David? The biblical text infers an almost immediate response on the part of King David to the news of Bathsheba's pregnancy. Had King David put together a plan in his mind during the days that soon followed his sexual intercourse with Bathsheba? Had it occurred to King David how he might need to rid himself of any religious or political problems were his adulterous actions to become openly public or yield a child?

King David faced several problems. Exodus 20:14 states, "Thou shalt not commit adultery." Secondly, Leviticus 20.10 states, "And the man that committeth adultery with another man's wife, even he that committeth adultery with his neighbour's wife, the adulterer and the adulteress shall surely be put to death."

Though scripture does not illuminate the breadth to which this knowledge of the King's adultery has spread through the city; it seems clearly plausible that the 'want-to-be' king Ahithophel would exploit and spread the gossip to his advantage in an effort to bring down King David. King David would have been well informed as to the rumors of his sexual tryst with Bathsheba circulating through his city and army. A cover-up is required, but what should King David do?

With a sentence of death now resting on King David's head what options does King David have to close the mouths of those who with evidence might make his adultery openly known to the nation? One option is the Bill and Hillary Clinton approach. King David could address the nation and straight out deny everything. "No, I did not have sex with that woman." Such a denial would deliver the full blame for her pregnancy upon Bathsheba. This course means the almost certain death of Bathsheba who suffers under the same death sentence punishment as David. King David through denial would also murder his child growing within Bathsheba.

What King David needs is a credible lie that may not pass the smell test, but with his position of authority makes challenging his word nearly impossible. There is no direct scriptural evidence that King David involves Bathsheba or informs Bathsheba of his plan. Providing Bathsheba with this cover provides her plausible deniability. Ahithophel, Bathsheba's grandfather, remains King

David's chief advisor and a powerful political player in the kingdom who could cause huge difficulties.

King David resolves that all he must do to have an adequate cover-up is to quickly get Uriah alone with Bathsheba for a night. This action would rid King David of responsibility to the pregnancy. Everyone would conclude Uriah to be the proud father of the newborn. It mattered little whether Uriah the Hittite had intercourse with Bathsheba during his brief visit; the visit itself provided King David cover. Following Uriah the Hittite's departure back to the battlefield King David would inquire of Bathsheba whether or not the visit had been conjugal. A conjugal visit would resolve the need for any further action on the part of King David, and David would have to watch his illegitimate son from afar.

In the event Uriah the Hittite's visit to his home was not a conjugal visit, Bathsheba and ultimately King David would be at risk for their adulterous act. Uriah the Hittite would of course know the child could not possibly be his child and Bathsheba would remain under a death sentence. It would be at this point that Uriah's death would be required to cover the sin and save King David's child. So if this scenario plays out King David will then engineer Uriah the Hittite's battlefield death. Bathsheba would be none the wiser of the King's murderous nature. Bathsheba would have plausible deniability and be able to mourn the battlefield death of her hero husband. King David would be regarded as the charitable King honoring his fallen trusted battlefield general by taking his widow for his own wife.

King David initiates his vile plan by calling Uriah back to the City of David for a battlefield report. Calling for the return to Jerusalem of a top seasoned battlefield leader for a field report had to raise eyebrows. Flipping a general into a messenger boy was an incredibly poor tactical decision and an insult to a battlefield commander. To all who had heard the rumors of King

David and Bathsheba no greater confirmation would be required as a legitimization of the rumors than Uriah the Hittite being pulled from the frontlines and sent home under the pretense of a menial task. Yet so intent is King David on covering his adultery, it is this hap hazardous plan he initiates.

Unfortunately, King David's plan to cover up his dirty deed assumed that Uriah the Hittite would respond in the same unprincipled fashion as the King is leading his life. As with any crime there is always a loose end that the fiendish plan fails to anticipate. King David has so long operated his life in the flesh and without the spiritual presences of God he fails to anticipate Uriah response in the light of his profoundly spiritual and honorable character.

The arc of the covenant and his army remain on the battlefield at the capitol city of the Ammonite people. The city's ancient biblical name is Rabbah or Rabbath. Today the ancient political center of the incest derived Ammonite people is the capital of modern Jordan and is called Amman. During the Hellenistic period the city was renamed Philadelphia. The total straight line distance from Jerusalem to Rabbah is about 46 miles. Men in those days did not travel in a straight line or on paved highways. The trek from the City of David and Ammon was a winding mountainous trail weaving its way as the topography allowed, so the distance by road is much longer and more difficult than the straight-line mileage might represent. It probably required a good two days to traverse the distance. These two days of solitary travel would provide an opportunity Uriah the Hittite to seek God's face for an answer to the sin that invaded his house and now envelopes him, his wife and his King.

In the midst of a great trial it is always difficult to understand why God chooses some men and women to carry great responsibility that to the human eye of understanding cries out unfair, not right, or why would a loving God do such a thing?

But Uriah the Hittite had been immersed in the scriptures as a temple servant known as the Nethinim. Uriah had descended from the Hittites who lived in Gibeon. These Hittites were Canaanite survivors of Joshua's purge of the Promise Land. These residents of Gibeon had been set apart by their faith filled choice to serve the one true God. Uriah has fulfilled God's charge to be a "servant of servants" which first starts as a water and wood carrier at tabernacle worship. Even now Uriah serves as a servant. Uriah serves King David's Army Commander Joab, so Uriah remains a servant of King David's servant Joab.

Uriah arrives in the City of David and reports to the King in his palace. The charade of a battlefield report is demanded of Uriah by King David. King David goes through the duties required of a King who has summoned home a battlefield general. King David does not care about the content of the report yet pretends to listens to Uriah. When King David thinks sufficient information has been asked of Uriah to fulfill the responsibility of an inclusive report, the other shoe that Uriah the Hittite anticipated, hits the floor.

2 Samuel 11:8 states, "And David said to Uriah, Go down to thy house, and wash thy feet. And Uriah departed out of the king's house, and there followed him a mess of meat from the king." (KJV)

Perhaps Uriah's thoughts are precursors to those of Esther who would follow in his footsteps years later. Esther faces a death sentence for doing a thing her husband King Xerxes (Ahasuerus) did not ask her to do. Esther acts for the sake of all her Jewish countrymen. Uriah the Hittite is to face a death sentence for not doing a thing his king requests. Uriah the Hittite will not yield to his earthly authority when it demands he deny his heavenly Authority. For the sake of his God, his king, his wife and his countrymen Uriah does not worship at David's table. In a foreshadowing of Shadrack, Meshach and Abednego, Uriah tells

King David that he will not worship the golden lie David has constructed.

In the book of Esther, Esther's Uncle Mordecai sends Esther a message. Esther is a Jew and Queen of Persia, but no one including the King knows her nationality. King Xerxes has been tricked by his chief advisor Haman the Agagite into issuing a proclamation and law that will result in the genocide of every Jew in all of Persia and Persia's territories. Queen Esther resides in a position that allows her actions to have a direct impact on the life or death of her people. Queen Esther faces her own mortality for actions that were not of her creation. Esther had merely been born of a race that others hated, yet she is now being challenged by her God to accept the role of a "living sacrifice", to put her needs second to the needs of others, to potentially die for others, to sacrifice her life to save others.

Mordecai, Queen Esther's uncle and family patriarch, commands Esther, "Do not think in your heart that you will escape in the king's palace any more than all the other Jews. For if you remain completely silent at this time, relief and deliverance will arise for the Jews from another place, but you and your father's house will perish. Yet who knows whether you have come to the kingdom for such a time as this?" (NKJV) Is this Uriah's final battlefield? Will Uriah the Hittite, after so many battles at King David's side, die by King David's hand? Will Uriah the Hittite die for taking a stand for the righteousness of God? Uriah answers these rhetorical thoughts like Queen Esther will answer them, "so I will go in unto the king…and if I perish, I perish."

Surely the irony of Genesis's record of Joseph's service in Potiphar's house did not go unconsidered by Uriah the Hittite on his long march from the battlefield to the City of David. Uriah understands that King David's attempt to hide his sin will almost certainly require the King to manipulate him into visiting his home and sleeping with his wife. Bathsheba will desire Uriah to lie with her just as Potiphar's wife desired Joseph to have a sexual liaison. In both Uriah's and Joseph's cases sin will be embraced through the act of sexual intercourse, and the gravity of refusing the sexual intercourse could quite possibly mean death.

It should be noted that Joseph makes no accusation against Potiphar or Potiphar's wife. In Potiphar's wife's accusation of Joseph, she accuses Joseph of mocking her. Uriah was soon to endure the mocking of King David who apparently considers him so lame as to swallow King David's subterfuge at face value. Uriah knew the penalty for standing for righteousness would be steep, but Uriah also knew the end of Joseph's story. Though thrown into prison Joseph's ordeal was followed with Genesis 39.21, "But the LORD was with Joseph, and showed him mercy, and gave him favor..." (KJV)

Uriah also remembers on his two day trek back to the City of David how David treated King Saul. When the young anointed David remained close to the Lord during the days King Saul pursued their small band, David had opportunity to end the trial of this long confrontation with King Saul by his own hand. Yet David said in 1Samuel 26:9-11, "Destroy him not: for who can stretch forth his hand against the LORD'S anointed, and be guiltless? David said furthermore, As the LORD liveth, the LORD shall smite him (King Saul); or his day shall come to die; or he shall descend into battle, and perish. The LORD forbid that I should stretch forth mine hand against the LORD'S anointed..." (KJV)

Uriah the Hittite would not seek to save himself by raising his voice or his hand against the anointed of God. Uriah will allow God to use him in His plan to convict King David of his sin even if it means sacrificing his wife, sacrificing any hope of having a family and heir, and sacrificing his very life and personal dreams in service to his God.

Uriah the Hittite is a battle hardened veteran with many years of service in the field. Uriah makes his report to King David. King David's response to Uriah's report is 2 Samuel 11:8 states, "And David said to Uriah, Go down to thy house, and wash thy feet. And Uriah departed out of the king's house, and there followed him a mess of meat from the king." (KJV)

King David is not concerned about the grit and grime that weeks of battlefield living has deposited on Uriah's person. David is not concern about the trail dust that covers Uriah's feet and legs. King David's concern for Uriah's personal hygiene is simply an encouragement for taking Bathsheba to bed. King David is quite sly in his encouragements. King David doesn't say Uriah you smell, so go take a shower and spend the night making love to your wife, but King David may have well said it.

The translation of 2 Samuel 11.8 leaves a bit to be desired. What is translated as "a mess of meat" when in reality the word is tribute. The tribute may well have been something much more alluring than a "mess of meat". The tribute might well have been a five course candlelight dinner for two with all the palace musicians playing softly in the background to set the mood. Whatever the tribute, "mess of meat" just doesn't do justice for the intended outcome.

Uriah the Hittite's heart must have been sickened. No matter how anticipated a personal disaster may be, actually living through the events tears at the soul. King David pats Uriah on the butt and tells him to hurry on down to his house and sleep with that cute little wife. All that floods Uriah's mind is, "It's true, every last piece of dirty gossip is true, my wife has cheated on me with my King." Uriah must have wanted to retch.

Uriah the Hittite resists the desire to run and hide from the shame of it all, and he refuses to go to his home as the King entices him to do. Knowing that a visit to his home would create the evil deception desired by King David, Uriah remains the faithful steadfast "servant of servants". The country is at war and Uriah will not sacrifice the camaraderie of his men's battlefield hardship. Uriah, the mighty man, sleeps on the ground amongst the men guarding the King's life, while the King is plotting to take his life.

The public effort Uriah embraces to allow all to see where he sleeps is in sharp contrast with King David's efforts to maintain the shroud of darkness over where it is he has slept. In a twist of irony Uriah the Hittite puts into practice the words of a Psalm King David has yet to write. King David would latter write in Psalm 27. 1-3, "The LORD is my light and my salvation; whom shall I fear? the LORD is the strength of my life; of whom shall I be afraid? When the wicked, even mine enemies and my foes, came upon me to eat up my flesh, they stumbled and fell. Though an host should encamp against me, my heart shall not fear: though war should rise against me, in this will I be confident." (KJV) It is the light of the Lord shining through Uriah's act of sleeping on the ground at King David's front door which in turn leads to the conviction of King David's heart.

No one can say just how many spies King David has watching every move of Uriah the Hittite following his departure from the presence of the King. King David wants a public confirmation from the mouths of many that Uriah entered into his own home. So King David would have had many of his servants tailing Uriah, but to their amazement they did not have to spy on Uriah. Uriah never attempts to elude David's men but remains openly in their presence. Uriah makes absolutely no effort to leave the King's house and visit Bathsheba.

Uriah wakes with a confidence and joy that indwells a faithful servant who has followed God's will for his life. Psalms 130:6 says, "My soul waiteth for the Lord more than they that watch for the morning: I say, more than they that watch for the morning." (KJV)

No such joy flood's King David's heart. Of one thing we can be certain, King David didn't sleep until late afternoon this morning. King David's breakfast is ruined with the report of his spies. Uriah did not do as you had hoped. He didn't go to his home. He did not sleep with his wife. Uriah never left our sides, and he slept amongst us as we guarded your palace.

One can only image the terror that befell these messengers as King David hurled his breakfast across the room. King David composes himself and revisits a contingency plan. He will find it necessary to implement the Ammonite gambit that arose out of the ashes of Sodom and Gomorrah. There appears to be no level of hypocrisy that King David will not sink to cover his adultery.

King David calls Uriah back into his presence later that day. King David has had time to collect his thoughts and regain his composure. Reading between the lines King David says to Uriah, "Look soldier, I brought you home from the battlefield. I had prepared for you and Bathsheba your wife a tremendously romantic evening, so what gives Uriah? Why didn't you receive my generosity and go home and enjoy this time with your wife?"

In a stunning rebuke of King David's current smutty lifestyle and indecent plan Uriah humbly says in 2 Samuel 11.11, "The ark, and Israel, and Judah, abide in tents; and my lord Joab, and the servants of my lord, are encamped in the open fields; shall I then go into mine house, to eat and to drink, and to lie with my wife? as thou livest, and as thy soul liveth, I will not do this thing." (KJV)

King David recognizes the spiritual resolve resident in Uriah while he prepares to mock Uriah's conviction and God's teaching. King David conceals the loathing seething within him generated by his vile pretense juxtaposed against the prophetic, simple and honest words spoken by God through his servant Uriah. In boxing terms King David is stunned by Uriah's punch, and he finds himself against the ropes sucking wind and biding his time hoping to catch a second wind. King David says, "Tarry here today also, and tomorrow I will let thee depart." So Uriah does as his King commands, and Uriah sits down in the middle of Jerusalem for all to see. The entire city will be his witness that he does not visit his home or his wife. Uriah remains visible to all Jerusalem until his summons arrives compelling him to return to the palace.

Years before an anointed David is running from the wrath of King Saul. David retreats to the town of Nob to a priest named Ahimelech. David lies to Ahimelech about being on a secret mission for King Saul. Under this pretense David requests provisions from the priest. Ahimelech answers David in 1 Samuel 21.4 saying, "There is no common bread undermine hand, but there is hallowed bread; if the young men have kept themselves at least from women." So it was not an unusual practice for soldiers on a King's mission to keep themselves as Uriah from sexual intercourse with their wives. Yet on his return to the palace King David's ploy will be the Ammonite gambit which was a product of the sinful behaviors practiced in Sodom and Gomorrah. King David's army is battling Ammon at this very moment, yet King David will attempt a final "hail Mary" play out of the Ammonite playbook in an attempt to loosen Uriah's resolve and get him in bed with Bathsheba.

The Ammonite gambit is the wicked tactic employed by Lot's daughters in an attempt to provide for their future through the energy of the flesh. Lot's daughters plied strong drink to their father Lot. The daughters' plan was to break the resolve of their father against having incestuous sexual intercourse with them through getting their dad drunk. In the case of Lot, his faculties and resolve were so diminished by drunkenness that his daughters are able to perform incestuous rape. Both daughters are impregnated as a result of having forced sex with their own father. The sons born to Lot's daughters are named Ammon and Moab. King David's army was encamped around Rabbah the capital city of the descendents of Ammon in an attempt to finally destroy what had risen from the ash heap of Sodom and Gomorrah. Unfortunately the vile spirit of the Ammonites was running wild in King David's heart and mind.

Upon his return to King David's palace the good times started to roll. Food and drink flowed freely. More than likely enticing dancers performed for the pleasure of the men present in an effort by King David to stimulate Uriah's sexual desires. Would Uriah's resolve melt away under the influence of the booze and possibly exotic dancers? Uriah knew full well what King David was attempting to accomplish. Though inebriated Uriah removes himself from the party and beds himself down in the same location he slept the previous night. The faithful servant soldier again sleeps at the King's door providing protection for his King. The Ammonite gambit fails.

King David has stated that he would allow Uriah to return to the battlefield. Uriah resolution not to sleep with his wife has demolished King David's scheme to get Uriah into his house and alone with Bathsheba. King David remains with a death sentence hanging over his head. King David doubles down with the fools' golden rule; do unto others before they have a chance to do unto you.

Uriah the righteous Hittite departs Jerusalem for Rabbah the next morning. King David entrusts sealed orders for his commanding general Joab into the hands of Uriah. Uriah need not soil his spiritual resolve by prying into Joab's orders. Just as Jesus did not find it necessary to expose Judas at the last supper to the remaining eleven disciples and just as Jesus repaired Peter's violence by healing the soldier's severed ear at his betrayal,

Uriah the Hittite need not open Joab's orders for he knew what the orders contained. Uriah knew King David would save himself, he knew his wife's only salvation from stoning was his death, and he knew he could not raise his hand or voice against the anointed of God. The orders contain Uriah's death sentence.

Chapter Twenty-four

What does a living sacrifice do when God requires the ultimate sacrifice of relinquishing one's life? Uriah the Hittite, the servant of servants, the dedicated soldier, the mighty man returns to God the precious gift of life with which God has entrusted him. The shedding of Uriah's blood will for a short time hide the sins of King David and wife Bathsheba.

Uriah the Hittite marches back to the battlefield knowing that his final confrontation with the enemy is drawing near.

In times where life seemingly allows us no control Psalm 23 is often visited. No one knows for certain when King David composed this psalm, but perhaps around one of those campfires in the years of King Saul's pursuit of David and his mighty men, David sang the psalm to his men as the Holy Spirit gave him utterance. Uriah may have heard these wonderful words flow from his friend David's lips the first time the world heard the wonderful song sung. "The LORD is my shepherd; I shall not want. He maketh me to lie down in green pastures: he leadeth me beside the still waters. He restoreth my soul: he leadeth me in the paths of righteousness for his name's sake. Yea, though I walk through the valley of the shadow of death, I will fear no evil: for thou art with me; thy rod and thy staff they comfort me. Thou preparest a table before me in the presence of mine enemies: thou anointest my head with oil; my cup runneth over. Surely goodness and mercy shall follow me all the days of my life: and I will dwell in the house of the LORD forever." (KJV)

How could any man sing such beautiful words if not anointed by God Uriah may have contemplated during the silence of his two day march back to the frontlines? "But why has all this burdensome pile of dung fallen on me Lord," Uriah may have cried out to the Lord. "What have I done to deserve this pain, shame and anguish? It is of course verse two of Psalm 23 that comes into play and is quite possibly the most difficult verse in the entire psalm.

Verse two of Psalm 23 contains the significant word "maketh." At times wayward lambs will stray from the fold and green pastures. After repeated wanderings the shepherd, for the safety of the lamb, will hobble the lamb forcing the lamb to lie down in green pastures. The lamb when hobbled cannot stray and stays close to the fold and to the shepherd. God does the same thing to those in his flock! Christians stray, and God pleads with them to return. God is not beyond utilizing the trials of life to hobble His children. God makes the Christian stay in the green pastures. Uriah had little understanding just how green this pasture is in which God the Father is allowing him to lie down.

Uriah arrives back at the front and enters Joab's camp. Uriah presents Joab the sealed orders. Joab reads the orders. King David "wrote in the letter, saying, Set ye Uriah in the forefront of the hottest battle, and retire ye from him, that he may be smitten, and die."

King David's order to Joab is unmistakable. King David wants Uriah dead. The King wants Uriah's death orchestrated to not appear as an out and out murder. King David wants the murder to appear as Uriah's death is the result of battlefield combat.

Today a method of suicide has been recognized by mental health practitioners. It is called suicide by cop. Individuals who haven't the will to pull the trigger and end their lives by their own hand will deliberately act in fashion that provokes a deadly response on the part of law enforcements officers. The individual engineers his or her own death, but the individual manipulates others into delivering the lethal strike.

King David in a complete and total abuse of his command authority orders Joab to place Uriah in harm's way within a battlefield situation and to leave him behind when all others are secretly called to retreat. It is a complete upending of "no man left behind." Leave Uriah behind and let the enemy kill him. Murder by the enemy is King David's resolution to his adultery. King David desires to limit the collateral damage his battlefield murder may cause, but it is acceptable to him that others may perish as a result of his scheme.

Flavius Josephus was a wealthy and educated Jew who ingratiated himself with a Roman named Vespasian who would later become Rome's emperor. Because of Josephus's relationship with the emperor he is given Roman citizenship with all the rights and privileges thereto appertaining. Josephus writes his famous work <u>The Antiquities of the Jews</u> for Roman and Greek consumption. Josephus records a relatively descriptive narration on the battlefield death of Uriah the Hittite.

"Upon this (Uriah's refusal to sleep with his wife) the king (David) was very angry at him; and wrote to Joab, and commanded him to punish Uriah, for he told him that he had offended him; and he suggested to him the manner in which he would have him punished, that it might not be discovered that he was himself the author of this his punishment; for he charged him to set him over against that part of the enemy's army where the attack would be most hazardous, and where he might be deserted, and be in the greatest jeopardy, for he bade him order his fellow soldiers to retire out of the fight. When he had written thus to him, and sealed the letter with his own seal, he gave it to Uriah to carry to Joab. When Joab had received it, and upon reading it understood the king's purpose, he set Uriah in that place where he knew the enemy would be most troublesome to them; and gave him for his partners some of the best soldiers in the army; and said that he would also come to their assistance with the whole army, that if possible they might break down

some part of the wall, and enter the city. And he desired him to be glad of the opportunity of exposing himself to such great pains, and not to be displeased at it, since he was a valiant soldier, and had a great reputation for his valor, both with the king and with his countrymen. And when Uriah undertook the work he was set upon with alacrity, he (Joab) gave private orders to those who were to be his (Uriah) companions, that when they saw the enemy make a sally, they should leave him. When, therefore, the Hebrews made an attack upon the city, the Ammonites were afraid that the enemy might prevent them, and get up into the city, and this at the very place whither Uriah was ordered; so they (Ammonites) exposed their best soldiers to be in the forefront, and opened their gates suddenly, and fell upon the enemy with great vehemence, and ran violently upon them. When those that were with Uriah saw this, they all retreated backward, as Joab had directed them beforehand; but Uriah, as ashamed to run away and leave his post, sustained the enemy, and receiving the violence of their onset, he slew many of them; but being encompassed round, and caught in the midst of them, he was slain, and some other of his companions were slain with him."

So Josephus fills in some of the blanks left by the eight verse that describe Uriah's death in the Old Testament text. King David is angry or puts on airs of anger at Uriah's refusal to go sleep with his wife Bathsheba. King David writes orders to his commanding general Joab with a rather detailed description of how he wants Uriah the Hittite murdered via a battlefield encounter. Joab, a murderer himself, sets himself to the task.

Uriah the Hittite's actions exude Godly motivation and character. Luke and Matthew in their descriptions of the actions and reactions to Christians and Christ living through them are a perfect reflection of Uriah the Hittite's life. Luke 6:22 says, "Blessed are ye, when men shall hate you, and when they shall separate you from their company, and shall reproach you, and cast out your name as evil, for the Son of man's sake." (KJV)

Standing for righteousness is never easy.

Matthew 5:43-48 says, "Ye have heard that it hath been said, Thou shalt love thy neighbour, and hate thine enemy. But I say unto you, Love your enemies, bless them that curse you, do good to them that hate you, and pray for them which despitefully use you, and persecute you; That ye may be the children of your Father which is in heaven: for he maketh his sun to rise on the evil and on the good, and sendeth rain on the just and on the unjust. For if ye love them which love you, what reward have ye? Do not even the publicans the same? And if ye salute your brethren only, what do ye more than others? do not even the publicans so? Be ye therefore perfect, even as your Father which is in heaven is perfect." (KJV)

Is it possible for Uriah to love King David with a greater love while David wallows in a cesspool of sin? Curse you, despitefully use you, hate you, persecute you, which of these phrases does not describe the treatment rendered Uriah by King David? Which of these descriptions does not describe the burden born by our Lord and Savior Jesus Christ by the hands of men?

As for King David his words perfectly reflect the wickedness in his heart betraying itself with his burning lips. Proverbs 26:23 says, "Burning lips and a wicked heart are like a potsherd covered with silver dross." (KJV) King David's actions are a public statement as to the condition of his heart. The Potter is about to take the clay pot that is David and breakdown that partially formed earthen vessel on His wheel with a mighty thump.

Proverbs 25 4-5 says in the New Living Translation, "Remove the impurities from silver, and the sterling will be ready for the silversmith. Remove the wicked from the king's court, and his reign will be made secure by justice." (NLV)

Removing dross from silver is not an action that will naturally occur. Without forceful intervention into King David's life the terrible evil that has run his life amuck will continue to manifest itself in blasphemous and sadistic fashion. When you let the devil ride, he is going to end up driving your life, and the devil is driving King David's life right off the cliff. But God has designed a methodology to remove this scum from King David's life. Dross is removed but the force of the refiner's fire. Unbeknownst to King David's blinded eyes, God has initiated the refining process.

Hebrews 12:28-29 shares, "Wherefore we receiving a kingdom which cannot be moved, let us have grace, whereby we may serve God acceptably with reverence and godly fear: For our God is a consuming fire." (KJV) King David is not acceptably serving God with reverence, godly fear and respect. David's lack of respect is about to unleash the consuming fire of God. Return to Chapter one Uriah's name translates as the "flame of the Lord". Since before time began, since before God created the first atom that would become the foundation of the world, God knew Uriah the Hittite. God had a plan for Uriah the Hittite's life. God provided Uriah with the perfect name for the ultimate task for which He designed his life. Uriah is to be the consuming flame of God that will strike the impurity, the dross, the scum from the heart of God's anointed and chosen King. Uriah is struck down and from out of the embers that remain of the ashes Uriah's flame springs a firestorm that consumes King David's sin and calls King David to repentance.

Uriah the Hittite and an elite group of soldiers are selected to proceed on a suicide mission against the besieged city of Rabbah. Rabbah is a city cut off from help. The city cannot be resupplied with food and provisions. The city's water supply will soon be compromised. Hunger and thirst will soon bring the city and its residents to capitulation. Yet Joab orders Uriah and the group of elite soldiers on an unnecessary and foolhardy frontal attack on the city's main gate. Further, Joab tells the elite unit of soldiers that would accompany Uriah to abandon Uriah to the enemy hordes when the counterattack comes, so Uriah will be killed.

Well, there are many idioms that probably passed through the minds of members of this elite group of soldiers and the army in general that day. Can you image a Navy Seal being asked by the commanding officer to leave a buddy on the field to be killed during a spurious military action? This action doesn't pass the smell test, someone is not playing with a full deck, who is asleep at the switch, I can't believe my ears, who has cracked under the strain, this is sketchy, really you are kidding, or somebody has rocks in their head and in the American military snafu would have passed through soldier's lips. Every soldier in that army recognized the malicious, malevolent and spiteful nature of this order. Every soldier has heard the rumors. Every soldier knows of Uriah's trip to Jerusalem. Every soldier is aware of Uriah's return with new orders. Every soldier knows it is an unjust execution disguised as a military action.

Uriah leads his men on a mission he knows would be his last. Any well trained military leader would have recognized what Joab ordered to be a suicide mission. Uriah's heart did not sink when his band of brothers deserted him on the field. But there remained a few faithful men, perhaps men Uriah had previously saved from death in the pitch of battle, who refuse Joab's devilish order and laid down their lives in the hope of saving their friend Uriah. Yet after a fierce battle that forever establishes the honor and character of Uriah and those that stood with him, the Ammonites prevail. Uriah's lifeless body is upon the ground. Uriah's life is not taken from him. Like any valiant soldier who dies in battle, he gives his life for king and country.

Joab dispatches a carefully crafted response to King David which covertly conveys to King David that his devious desires have been dutifully dispatched. The mission is accomplished. David religiously waits for Bathsheba to complete a respectable mourning period for the death of her husband before snatching her into his house as his wife. At last the sordid little affair is behind King David. King David's misuse of his anointing to cover his sin is an affront to God. King David believes he has muted the bad press that has spun out of control since rumors of his illicit dalliance first hit the streets months earlier. The story fades from the front page and the angry crowd acquiesces to a man made rewrite of the truth. But God knows the truth and the other shoe will fall.

Proverbs 28:13 states, "People who conceal their sins will not prosper, but if they confess and turn from them, they will receive mercy." (KJV) The "flame of the Lord" will rise up and consume King David's concealed sin.

Chapter Twenty-five

After adultery with his wife, after making a mockery of Uriah's righteous stand, after murdering Uriah on the battlefield King David honors Uriah's death well died, but God honors Uriah's life well lived.

Uriah has been absence from his earthly life for six and perhaps as many as nine months. King David remains hunkered down in his palace satisfied that his sin will remain uncovered. Public opinion is no longer focused on the rumors surrounding Uriah's death. King David is married to Bathsheba, and she has taken her place alongside all of King David's other wives and concubines. The seared heart of King David shows no sign of remorse or penitence for the heinous crimes he has committed.

Proverbs 16:9 states, "A man's heart deviseth his way: but the LORD directeth his steps." (KJV) King David's thoughts, planning, calculating and imaginations carry him on a destructive journey of moral disintegration. King David does what is right in his own eyes. David accomplishes what he thought is most self serving, but little did King David realize that a "then suddenly" of God is about to redirect his steps.

Uriah the Hittites remains are moldering in the grave. Natural decay is disintegrating what remains of his natural body. His wife Bathsheba has taken another to be her husband. No natural heir remains to carry on his name and heritage. No legacy of his existence remains in this world save what God is about to resurrect.

Uriah the Hittite is an honest, pious and earnest man. Despite all the vileness heaped on him by King David, he remains faithful. Uriah loves his King. Uriah surely prays for his king. In Uriah's heart are words yet to be spoken, "But I say unto you, Love your enemies, bless them that curse you, do good to them that hate you, and pray for them which despitefully use you, and persecute you; That ye may be the children of your Father which is in heaven."

Uriah, while sleeping at the King's door his last two nights in Jerusalem surely prays for his master to be free from sin's bondage that has engulfed his life. Uriah's life well lived will return from the grave to convict King David of his sin.

Nathan is a prophet and friend of King David. Nathan has a respected history with King David, and when God finds the time right He delivers a spiritual awakening to King David through Nathan.

Proverbs 16:14 says, "The wrath of a king is as messengers of death: but a wise man will pacify it." Nathan knows the evil that is tearing apart the King's heart. God provides Nathan with a story to share with the King. Nathan knows full well God's intent is to provide conviction that will produce a penitent heart in David. The story God provides has four characters: a wandering traveler, an extremely rich man, a very poor man and a ewe-lamb. King David is familiar with being rich as well as being poor, and as a shepherd boy alone at night caring for his flock David knows the love and attachment a shepherd can have for a favorite pet ewe-lamb.

Some Jewish scholars identify the wandering man as King David's yetzer hara. Yetzer hara is the inner base tendency's that will propel a man or woman to incline their heart to engage in the self gratification of fleshly desires. But these evil inclinations for a Christian merely represent the fallen nature of man seeking opportunity to exert itself. The opportunity for the flesh to exert itself over a faith filled response empowered by the Holy Spirit manifests at the moment of temptation.

John 15:5 states, "I am the vine, ye are the branches: He that abideth in me, and I in him, the same bringeth forth much fruit: for without me ye can do nothing." So the Word shares in Matthew 26:41, "Watch and pray, that ye enter not into temptation: the spirit indeed is willing, but the flesh is weak." In Luke 22:40 Jesus says to his disciples, "Pray that ye enter not into temptation." Yet Christ returns to his disciples after a short time. "And when he (Jesus) rose up from prayer, and is come to his disciples, he found them sleeping for sorrow, and said unto them, Why sleep ye? rise and pray, lest ye enter into temptation."

Sleep in its proper roll restores the human body, but sleep as avoidance is an attempt to escape the challenges of a faith-filled Christian walk. Sleeping your troubles away never works. Jesus in Gethsemane prayed His way through sorrow while the disciples faithlessly escaped their sorrows through sleep. The flesh will use any manner of human weakness to avoid the pain of sorrow. People eat too much or not enough, drink too much, have sex too much in an effort to assuage the burden of their pain through the satisfaction of their lusts.

Where is King David found when he falls into sexual temptation with Bathsheba? David is sleeping too much, eating too much, drinking too much and praying too little. 1Corinthians 10:13 says, "There hath no temptation taken you but such as is common to man: but God is faithful, who will not suffer you to be tempted above that ye are able; but will with the temptation also make a way to escape, that ye may be able to bear it." The enemy of our soul watches and waits for these opportunities to strike at our hearts. 1 Peter 5:8 says, "Be sober, be vigilant; because your adversary the devil, as a roaring lion, walketh about, seeking whom he may devour:" King David is not prepared when the wandering traveler arrived for a visit.

King David is, of course, the rich man in the story God provides Nathan. Uriah the Hittite reappearing from the grave is the poor man, and the ewe lamb represents Bathsheba. At this point in his life King David is indeed a very rich man when the traveler comes for a visit. David has every ability to satisfy his sexual lusts within the confines his own house. King David has 6 wives and 10 concubines with which to have intercourse, but to satisfy his appetite David finds it necessary to violate God's law and another man's wife.

The murder of Uriah is omitted in this story, but God fills in a few of the missing pieces of Uriah's life. The poor man is living with his children which infers that Uriah may have previously lost a family perhaps during the Gibeon genocide. The poor man attempts to replace lost affection and companionship with a ewe lamb Bathsheba who grows up with the poor man and his children. Yet when the traveler arrives restraint is thrown to the wind, and King David will reap the whirlwind. King David devours the ewe lamb leaving the house of Uriah the Hittite in utter ruin through the misuse of God's blessings.

At the completion of Nathan's story King David is outraged. "The lady doth protest too much, methinks," Queen Gertrude answers Shakespeare's Hamlet. Often times when someone is aggressively insistent about the remediation of an indignity done, it is the consequence of their own actions coming home to roost. Such grand pronouncements seem to be a balm to a seared conscience when consequences are for their like sin falling on another. King David has married the women he defiled and murdered her husband in a cover-up. This act is an affront to the sanctity of marriage and diminishes the severity of the crimes. King David has successfully polluted a house that God established.

King David denounces the rich man's actions. The king passes judgment on the rich man and orders that a four-fold restitution be made. Because of the truly aggravated nature of the rich man's crime, because his cold and callus act is simply for self gratification, because there is within the resources entrusted this the rich man the ability to satisfy the needs of the traveler King David condemns the rich man to death. King David's judicial sentence of the rich man extends a judgment that is far heavier than the Levitical law requires.

Levitical law requires a life for a life and a beast for a beast. Leviticus 24:21 states, "And he that killeth a beast, he shall restore it: and he that killeth a man, he shall be put to death." Leviticus 24.22 also states, "Ye shall have one manner of law, as well for the stranger, as for one of your own country: for I am the LORD your God." King David exceeds the demands of the law when pronouncing a punishment that in turn falls upon his own head.

Nathan then tells King David that he is the rich man. The identification of David as the guilty party brings wave after wave of conviction into David's heart. God shares the simple truth of His word in a punishment for David and his house. What you have sown David, so shall you reap. Violence will not depart from David's house, what David had attempted to cover up I will reveal to all in the bright light of day, and for Uriah's life God requires one life, the life of the child born out of adultery with Bathsheba.

King David's ungodly four-fold restitution will plague and curse his own house. King David not only loses the infant son born to Bathsheba, but he will lose three more sons through violence within his own house. The second of David's sons who dies a violent death is Amnon.

Amnon is King David's eldest son born of his first wife Ahinoam who came from the town of Jezreel. Amnon loved his half-sister whose name is Tamar who is the daughter of King David's third wife Maachah. Third wife Maachad is also the mother of Absalom who is King David's third son.

Amnon so desired Tamar that with the help of his cousin devised a plan to force himself on Tamar. Amnon made himself sick. When his father King David visited him, Amnon convinced David to allow Tamar to attend to his illness. While Tamar is tending to Amnon, Amnon rapes her. In one of the most prophetic statements on premarital sex in the Bible, 2 Samuel 13:14-15 reports, "Howbeit he would not hearken unto her voice: but, being stronger than she, forced her, and lay with her. Then Amnon hated her exceedingly; so that the hatred wherewith he hated her is greater than the love wherewith he had loved her. And Amnon said unto her, Arise, be gone."

So the violence of rape is committed by King David's eldest son on his half-sister. Absalom, Tamar's full brother, recognizes what has happened and plans his revenge. Absalom, like his father who engaged Joab to execute Uriah's battlefield murder, engages his servants to murder his half brother Amnon at a large family party. Amnon becomes the second of King David's sons to die, and this death is a violent death.

Absalom, following the murder of his half brother, spent the next several years building support for his kingship. Absalom stages a coup d'état moving to forcibly place himself on his elderly father's throne. As Nathan's prophetic message stated, "Behold, I will raise up evil against thee out of thine own house, and I will take thy wives before thine eyes, and give them unto thy neighbour, and he shall lie with thy wives in the sight of this sun." (KJV) King David flees Jerusalem in advance of the coup d'etat leaving behind his ten concubines to care for the palace. Absalom enters King David's palace and with the council of Ahithophel, Bathsheba's grandfather, sets up a tent on the palace roof where all Jerusalem could see. Absalom then under the tent systematically rapes all of his father's concubines "in the sight of the sun" and before all the eyes of Jerusalem. The coup d'etat fails and Absalom meets his violent end at the hands of Joab,

King David's servant, who is the King David's fellow conspirator in the murder of Uriah.

King David's last son to die a violent death is Adonijah. Adonijah is next in line for the throne in a hereditary hierarchy when King David is dying. Adonijah has himself proclaimed King, but King David on his death bed announces Solomon to be his heir. Adonijah begs and is granted forgiveness for his actions.

Adonijah attempts a second time to gain the throne. Adonijah approaches King Solomon's mother Bathsheba. By this time Bathsheba had spent years contemplating every possible religious and political pathway to the throne for her son Solomon and David's other male heirs. Bathsheba is well aware of the intrigue afoot in King Solomon's court.

Adonijah comes to Bathsheba with a proposition where the confession of true love is merely a cover to gain the great inheritance of Israel's throne. Adonijah confesses a desire to take Abishag the Shunammite to be his wife. Abishag the Shunammite is the last of King David's concubines. She had been supplied to King David on his death bed in an attempt to restore his health. But even the fair Abishag could not restore King David, and the Bible clearly states he knew her not, that is King David did not have conjugal relations with Abishag the Shunammite.

Adonijah greatly underestimates the astuteness of Bathsheba's understanding of the political and religious precedents resident in Adonijah's request. Bathsheba knew full well that Adonijah through this request is positioning himself for a second attempt to take the throne from her son Solomon. Rather than act with a forgiving spirit and deny Adonijah's request and rebuke him for his foolishness, Bathsheba grant's Adonijah's request which she knows will require King Solomon to execute his half-brother. Rather than writing down a death sentence as King David did with Uriah, Bathsheba out of her own motives and out of her own mouth delivers what she knows is a death sentence for Adonijah. Bathsheba is forcing her son King Solomon to kill his brother Adonijah.

Upon delivery of the request Bathsheba receives a stunning rebuke from her son. King Solomon in the New Living Bible translations says, "How can you possibly ask me to give Abishag to Adonijah?" King Solomon demanded. "You might as well ask me to give him the kingdom! You know that he is my older brother, and that he has Abiathar the priest and Joab son of Zeruiah on his side." Well, Bathsheba knew that Abiathar and Joab allied themselves with Adonijah. Unwilling to trust the protection of her son to God's hands Bathsheba took measures into her own hands.

King Solomon is compelled to execute his brother Adonijah because of Bathsheba's actions. It is within Bathsheba's power to talk some good sense into Adonijah and put a stop to Adonijah's plot before someone has to die, but she had learned to well from King David. Violence is in Bathsheba's heart.

King David, now dead, loses a fourth son to a violent death. King Solomon has his half-brother Adonijah executed for plotting against the throne. King David's self imposed four-fold punishment is complete. Uriah the Hittite through his own self-sacrifice provides King David the message God uses to draw David to repentance. King David's sin continues to extract its cost after King David's death while Uriah's self sacrifice continues to be rewarded.

Chapter Twenty-six

Uriah's blessing from Christ, "The last shall be first and the first shall be last."

Mar 10:29-31 states, "And Jesus answered and said, Verily I say unto you, There is no man that hath left house, or brethren, or sisters, or father, or mother, or wife, or children, or lands, for my sake, and the gospel's, But he shall receive an hundredfold now in this time, houses, and brethren, and sisters, and mothers, and children, and lands, with persecutions; and in the world to come eternal life. But many that are first shall be last; and the last first."

Uriah the Hittite in his fulfillment of his charge, to be a servant of servants, lies down his life for the anointed of God. Uriah willingly gives up the keys to his house, he willingly gives up all the worldly relationships that life can provide, he willingly gives up his wife, children and worldly possession for service to God's anointed, and he willingly gives up control of his life.

The apostle Paul says in 1Co 15:10, "But by the grace of God I am what I am: and his grace which was bestowed upon me was not in vain; but I laboured more abundantly than they all: yet not I, but the grace of God which was with me." (KJV) God provides the grace that allows us to meet the persecutions that come in life. Christ did so with Paul, and He did so with Uriah the Hittite.

1 Peter 2:20-23 proclaims, "For what glory is it, if, when ye be buffeted for your faults, ye shall take it patiently? But if, when ye do well, and suffer for it, ye take it patiently, this is acceptable with God. For even hereunto were ye called: because Christ also suffered for us, leaving us an example, that ye should follow his steps: Who did no sin, neither was guile found in his mouth: Who, when he was reviled, reviled not again; when he suffered,

he threatened not; but committed himself to him that judgeth righteously." (KJV)

There is no sin to be laid upon Uriah throughout this biblical account. Uriah is not buffeted for sins of his own doing. Uriah suffers all patiently which is acceptable to God because Uriah through the grace extended him endures his persecution to the very end of life itself. The sweet savor of his offering is acceptable to God.

Commendation extended by great and powerful men are frequently sought out and cherished in this world. Christ's disciples even squabbled amongst themselves who would be first in line. A worldly legacy can well be established with words of commendation spoken by a king or other high placed dignitaries.

So King David, as death approaches, chooses to extend such commendations to those that served him well through his life in a codicil to his last will and testament. King David systematically goes through the list of worthy warriors and many of their battlefield exploits in 2 Samuel Chapter 23. The list is filled with thirty-six mighty men who killed many of King David's enemies.

The thirty-seventh and last mighty man mentioned is Uriah the Hittite. Last on David's list to be honored is the one soldier and friend who should have been first. Though Uriah had many battlefield exploits, none were mentioned in King David's accounting. How could King David in his last earthly opportunity to honor Uriah only find it within himself to mention his name?

Of the thirty-seven who heroically battled King David's enemies there remains only one amongst the thirty-seven who was killed by King David's enemies or more truthfully by King David himself. Of the thirty-seven willing to die for King David, there is only one who actually dies for his King and country.

Even at the end of his life, King David is unable to publicly confess for posterity the evil he perpetrated against his friend. It seems all King David can do is barely mutter Uriah's name as almost an afterthought. Uriah deserved so much more from King David, but it remains more the reason we live for Christ and not earthly accolades.

One thousand years pass before Uriah the Hittite's name reappears in scriptures. 2 Peter 3:8 provides insight into the inner workings of God's clock, "But, beloved, be not ignorant of this one thing, that one day is with the Lord as a thousand years, and a thousand years as one day." (KJV)

Christ carries Uriah's sacrifice for 1000 years, yet for Christ Uriah's sacrifice was just over 24 hours old.

The last mention of Uriah's name is in the New Testament's first book of Matthew written 1000 years after Uriah's death. The Book of Matthew is written in Hebrew and is intended for a Jewish audience. The Jewish audience is knowledgeable in Hebrew history. The Jewish reader has been taught since a tender age of the nation's famous King David and King Solomon. The reader is aware of King David's failings with Bathsheba.

So why does Matthew 1.6 say, "And Jesse begat David the king; and David the king begat Solomon of her that had been the wife of Urias;" (KJV) Did Christ suddenly forget Bathsheba's name? No, Christ is the only man who has ever lived who was able to personally select his heritage. Christ wanted all to remember Uriah the Hittite. It was now time for the new covenant with the Jew and with the Gentile. A new covenant that is epitomized through the life Uriah the Hittite lived; a new covenant that is epitomized by the living sacrifice of its followers.

This covenant demands the just to live by faith. Making yourself available without eating from the tree of the knowledge of good and evil is a difficult task, but it is the task of a living sacrifice.

In closing please you allow me a bit of literary freedom and a great deal of imagination. I have one last story regarding spiritual heritages that could be considered initially quite unfair treatment of men who dedicated their life to serving the Lord.

It is often impossible for us to comprehend God weaving his wonderful tapestry as our life casqued through time. Often it is only looking back at the volume of God's work that human eyes can recognize God's faithfulness.

Reginald Heber was born on April 21, 1783 in Malpas, Cheshire, England. Heber was a missionary who worked in Calcutta, India. More than 100 years prior to the arrival of an Albanian named Anjeze Gonxhe Bejaxhia, who would become known as Mother Teresa, Heber labored to bring Christ to that sub-continent. On April 3, 1826 in obscurity at Trichinipoly, Tamil Nadu, India Heber died of a cerebral hemorrhage.

Heber had written hymns but not one was ever published during his life. After his death about 57 of his pieces were printed in 1827.

John Bacchus Dykes was born on March 10 1823 at Kingston upon Hull, England. Dykes labored for the Lord in small parishes and died on January 22, 1876 in relative obscurity at Ticehurst, Sussex, England.

Dykes was a church organist that became vicar of St Oswald's church in Durham England. One of his best tunes came with the birth of his son, and he named both the tune and his son St Oswald. I guess being John St. Oswald Dykes, was better than John Bacchus Dykes for who in church work would really favor being named after Bacchus the Roman god of strong drink and intoxication.

"I looked for a man among them who would build up the wall and stand before me in the gap," says Ezekiel 22:30. (NIV)

On October 4, 1997, a group known as "Promise Keepers" hosted "*Stand in the Gap: A Sacred Assembly of Men*" on the National Mall in Washington, D.C. Conservative estimates put the size of the gathering between 1.5 and 2.2 million men. Arguably it was the largest assembly of godly men since Moses led Israel out of Egypt.

On that day John Dykes was kicking around his mansion in glory and there was a knock on his door. The messenger said the King of Kings and Lord of Lords request your presence for a concert featuring one of your works. John Dykes scratches his head and says I've been in heaven for 121 years. Nobody much listened to my tunes when I was on the earth. I wonder what this could be about? So he departs with the messenger.

Across town the same event is repeated at Reginald Heber mansion. The messenger said the King of Kings and Lord of Lords request your presence for a concert featuring one of your works. Heber tells the messenger he wasn't sure he understood, he had only written the words to a handful of hymns and no one ever sang them much when he was on the earth, and none were ever published while he was alive. He too wondered what was up, but he quickly departed with the messenger.

John and Reginald both arrived at the same time and were ushered into Christ's presence.

Jesus greets them and says, "Today the world tells you if you get two million people buying one of your songs it's a great thing, and the world will make you rich. In my economy gentlemen, you can be long forgotten on earth, but John I remember you faithfully hearing and transcribing the melody I placed in your heart that day in 1862 when your son was born. Reginald I can still remember you scribbling down the words to the hymn I gave you for your Trinity Sunday service in 1826. Thank you both for faithfully recording the passion I shared with your hearts.

Now won't you join me in a concert featuring your faithfulness? With John to his left and Reginald to his right the King of Kings and Lord of Lords sweeps his arm through space and the portals of heaven open. Looking down John says that is the St. Oswald melody I hear, and Reginald says I hear the words to the Trinity Sunday hymn here in heaven.

Yes, Jesus responds, it is the Promise Keeper meeting on the mall in Washington, DC. It is easy to get 2 million people to listen to a song one at a time but because of your faithfulness there are 2 million voices piercing heaven singing in unison that one song I gave you. Enjoy the concert, great is your reward.

I looked for a man among them who would build up the wall and stand before me in the gap.

Are you willing to stand in the gap, are you willing to give away that godly smile, are you willing to give a godly gift as did the good Samaritan, are you willing to give a few hours of methodical study and prayer so when someone near you has a question you can speak an answer with God voice?

Through all the trials and tribulations life presents let us not hesitate at the Brook of Besor. Let us choose cheerfulness no matter the cost. Let us become the living sacrifice. Let us join in

Reginald Heber and John Dykes in the hymn that shook heaven long after they lie moldering in the grave. Let's sing:

Holy, holy, holy! Lord God Almighty!
Early in the morning our song shall rise to Thee;
Holy, holy, holy, merciful and mighty!
God in three Persons, blessèd Trinity!

Holy, holy, holy! All the saints adore Thee,
Casting down their golden crowns around the glassy sea;
Cherubim and seraphim falling down before Thee,
Who was, and is, and evermore shall be.

Holy, holy, holy! though the darkness hide Thee,
Though the eye of sinful man Thy glory may not see;
Only Thou art holy; there is none beside Thee,
Perfect in power, in love, and purity.

Holy, holy, holy! Lord God Almighty!
All Thy works shall praise Thy Name, in earth, and sky, and sea;
Holy, holy, holy; merciful and mighty!
God in three Persons, blessèd Trinity!.

Gen 15:1 says, "After these things the word of the LORD came unto Abram in a vision, saying, Fear not, Abram: I am thy shield, and thy exceeding great reward." (KJV) Our reward is not something of this earthly plan. Our reward is not of riches and wealth. Our exceedingly great reward is God's gift of Himself in our salvation. All earthly desires should pale and fall away in service to the King who allows us life through the very air that we breathe. Uriah the Hittite knew and understood his exceedingly great reward and willingly yielded all his desires to his Sovereign as his thank you to his God and King.

Bibliography

Barnhouse, Donald Grey, *(1965) The Invisible War*, Zondervan Publishing House.
Frost, Robert, *(1916), "The Road Not Taken.*
Henry, M. *(2008) Matthew Henry Commentary on the Whole Bible,* Hendrickson Publishing.
KJV (1611,1769) The Authorized Version or King James Version Outside of the United Kingdom, the KJV is in the public domain.
NLV (2008) New Living Bible, Tyndale House Publishers.
NKJV (1975), The New King James Version, Thomas-Nelson Publishers
Sprague, W. B. *(1839). The Life and Sermons of Edward D. Griffin.* Carlisle, PA: First Banner of Truth edition 1987.
Strong, J. *(1997) Strong's Exhaustive Concordance of the Bible,* Thomas Nelson Incorporated.
Thomas, M. I. *(1961). The Saving Life of Christ,* Zondervan Publishing House
Thomas, M. W. *(1964). The Mystery of Godliness.*: Zondervan Publishing House.

www.ingramcontent.com/pod-product-compliance
Lightning Source LLC
Chambersburg PA
CBHW032106090426
42743CB00007B/257